The History
of Czechs
in Cedar Rapids

Volume I
1852 – 1942

and

Volume II
1942 - 1982

Edited by
Donna Merkle

Revised 2012
Czech Heritage Foundation
P.O. Box 8476
Cedar Rapids, Iowa 52408

Foreword to the 2012 Revised Edition

When the Floods of 2008 hit the city of Cedar Rapids, many businesses suffered irreparable damage. One such casualty was the printing company that had produced the original two volumes of *The History of Czechs in Cedar Rapids*. Gone was the shop, gone were the printing plates, and gone was all the artwork to produce those plates.

But out of this loss there arose a fantastic opportunity. New technology employing digital masters was rendering the old printing process obsolete. Flood or no flood, it would have been necessary to upgrade to this new standard. And the need to replenish our inventory of copies available for sale created the perfect opportunity to implement some changes to the original manuscripts that I believe are improvements as well.

The first section of *The History of Czechs in Cedar Rapids*, covering the years 1852-1942, was originally published in two parts in *The Iowa Journal of History and Politics* in 1944. This scholarly work was written by Martha E. Griffith in partial fulfillment of the requirements for her Master of Arts degree in history from the University of Wyoming in 1942. The two parts printed in *The Iowa Journal of History and Politics* were combined into *The History of Czechs in Cedar Rapids, Volume I* by the Czech Heritage Foundation of Cedar Rapids. The format of this volume has been preserved in order to maintain the detail contained in the footnotes. Diacritical markings have been added to the Czech names of the organizations (but not individuals) in order to make them more true to the original Czech spelling and to match the standard adopted by the authors of the second volume.

The History of Czechs in Cedar Rapids, Volume II covers the years 1942-1982. This volume was prepared by a committee on behalf of the Czech Heritage Foundation of Cedar Rapids, with input from many individuals in the Czech community. Many of these voices are silent now. I have preserved the format of the second volume so that the reader can sense the labor of love and pride that went into its creation.

While the second volume in its original printing did not follow the same scholarly structure of Volume I, it did contain a very important scholarly feature. It had an index. Actually, it had four indexes: a subject index for Volume I, a name index for Volume I, a subject index for Volume II, and a name index for Volume II. Unfortunately, the benefits of the two indexes for Volume I were lost on those who did not possess a copy of that volume.

Consequently, there were three compelling reasons to combine the two volumes into one book: (1) both volumes needed to be reprinted; (2) both volumes needed to be digitalized in order to be printed according to current standards; and (3) it would be beneficial to have both volumes and their indexes contained in a single printed work. I did make three modifications, however. First of all, I combined all four indexes into one. Secondly, in some instances, I expanded the number of citations for a specific reference. The third change needs a little explanation.

One feature that the two subject indexes had in common was to combine entries under major headings. But sometimes an entry would be listed under one heading in Volume I and a different heading in Volume II. Besides creating confusion, this structure was awkward and difficult to use. I believe a reader's first impulse is to look up a specific reference by its own name, not the category to which it might belong. But I also think it is valuable to be able to review a categorical list to see all of the entries in a particular subject area. My goal was to find a solution that was not only logical and easy to use, but also preserved what the committee had intended with their original concept. I settled on a two-part solution to this problem. A new combined general index allows the reader to find a specific subject or topic under its own entry. For those seeking a comprehensive list based on category, I have extracted those lists from the former indexes and placed them in their own Appendix.

I hope that the reader will find that this 2012 edition of *The History of Czechs in Cedar Rapids* not only provides improvements over the prior separate volumes but also will serve as a valuable resource for historical or genealogical research.

I would like to thank the board of directors of the Czech Heritage Foundation of Cedar Rapids for allowing me to prepare this new edition of *The History of Czechs in Cedar Rapids*. I would especially like to thank Karen Lehmann, current editor of the Czech Heritage Foundation's quarterly newsletter, for designing the cover and for assisting in preparing the manuscript for publication.

I would also like to thank everyone who helped me by answering my numerous questions. Every answer allowed me to proceed with greater confidence and ease.

Donna Merkle
March 2012
Cedar Rapids, Iowa

Table of Contents

The History
of Czechs
in Cedar Rapids

Volume I
1852 - 1942

by

Martha E. Griffith

Reprinted from
The Iowa Journal of History and Politics
Courtesy of:
Division of the State Historical Society
Iowa City, Iowa

Foreword

In 1944 Martha Eleanor Griffith, a veteran teacher at Wilson High School in the Czech district of Cedar Rapids, prepared two penetrating articles on the Czech population of her city and published them in the State Historical Society's *Iowa Journal of History and Politics*. To this day these articles stand as authoritative in their subject area. With this edition Griffith will reach the wider readership she deserves.

The strongest sections of the articles deal with Czech strivings to perpetuate their heritage in an American setting. Ironically, efforts in this direction more often than not utilized Yankee style organizations. Griffith found "nothing" in the European heritage to account for the dozens of organizations which sprang up here for the perpetuation of Czech values. Resorting to Yankee techniques may have done more in the way of Americanizing the Czechs of Cedar Rapids than for the avowed purpose of maintaining Czech distinctiveness.

A fitting tribute both to the Czech community and to Griffith would be for an able historian to pick up where she left off. For example, why was it that the Protestant Czechs tended to hold on to their native language more tenaciously than did the Catholic Czechs? What were the types and intensities of responses in "the Bohemian Athens of America" when Germany occupied Czechoslovakia in the late 1930s? How the people of Czech descent zealously pressured the government of the United States for action during more recent strivings for freedom and self determination in the Old Country? These and many other questions deserve to be answered.

Reading Griffith will acquaint people with the valiant strivings of the Czechs back to the time of Jan Hus and cause Americans to raise their heads for taking this element into their population. I encourage Iowans to continue to support *The Iowa Journal of History and Politics* which published Martha Griffith's articles originally in 1944.

Peter T. Harstad, Director
Iowa State Historical Department
Division of the State Historical Society

Introduction

My sister, Martha Griffith, was a native of Cedar Rapids and spent most of her life in this community. She was educated in the Cedar Rapids schools, attending old Madison and Polk Elementary Schools. Martha was a 1912 graduate of old Washington High School. In 1916 she received her B.A. degree from Coe College, majoring in history. Martha attended summer school sessions at the University of Iowa, the University of Colorado, and earned her M.A. degree from the University of Wyoming in the summer of 1942. After four years of teaching in small Iowa towns, Martha joined the staff of the Cedar Rapids schools. With the exception of one year, she taught in this community from 1920 until her retirement in 1959.

In 1920 Martha was assigned to teach Social Studies at the old Van Buren School which, at that time, served as the junior high school for the southwest section of Cedar Rapids. When Wilson Junior High was completed in 1925, the Van Buren faculty moved there. Martha spent the rest of her teaching experience at Wilson.

Over fifty years ago, when Martha first taught in Cedar Rapids, the southwest section of the city was largely a Czech community. Since many parents could not speak English, it was necessary to have some Czech teachers on the faculty. My sister did not qualify in this respect. I used to tell her that I couldn't understand how she could possibly have taught in southwest Cedar Rapids for almost 40 years and not be able to speak a word of Czech.

During summer school sessions in the late 1930s and 1940s, Martha worked on her graduate studies at the University of Wyoming. When it came time to select a topic for her thesis, she decided to write about the history of the Czech people in Cedar Rapids. She began her research in the fall of 1941. During the last part of the 1942 spring semester, Martha took a leave of absence in order to finish this work. The thesis was written in the summer of 1942 at which time she received her M.A. degree.

Since Martha could neither read nor speak Czech, she encountered many problems. Records which she needed were written only in the Czech language. But the Czech people in the community were most helpful and many contributed a great deal of time and effort to this project. I regret that it is impossible for me to note the names of all who helped. This was many years ago and I did not know most of these individuals. However, one name does stand out. Without the help of the late Annette Cypra Thomas (Mrs. Tom Thomas), Martha would never have been able to secure the information she needed.

Thus the thesis "The Czechs in Cedar Rapids" was not the result of Martha's efforts alone. She always felt that it was really the contribution of all the wonderful Czech people in Cedar Rapids.

Ruth Griffith
Grinnell, Iowa

Ancestry

The Czechs[1] are descendants of an ancient Slavic tribe, which migrated in the fifth century from the region of the Vistula River to the central part of the European continent. According to legend, they were guided there by a chieftain named Cechus, or Cech. The Romans, who had previously found the Alpine Boii tribe living in that area, had designated it Boio-hemia, or Bohemia, but to speak of the Slavic occupants of Bohemia as Bohemians is fallacious; that term refers to French gypsies. It is preferable to designate the inhabitants of Bohemia as Czechs.[2]

The history of the Czechs from the fifth to the seventeenth century is a record of recurring wars with German and Magyar invaders. The culmination of their struggle came with their defeat by the Habsburgs in the Battle of White Mountain on November 8, 1620. This battle marked the termination of Bohemia's independence as a nation and the subsequent collapse of Protestantism. As a result, some thirty-six thousand families went into exile. It is not known how many of these exiles came to America, but it is certain that Augustine Herrman, who arrived in New York in 1633, and Frederick Philipse (Vrederych Felypsen), who came to that same colony in 1647, were the first Czechs to come to America.[3]

It was not, however, until about 1848 that the Czechs began to emigrate to the United States to any marked extent. One of the economic causes for this emigration was the discovery of gold in California, mention of which appeared in

[1] The spelling "Cech" was used prior to 1918, but the present form, "Czech", has been used in this manuscript except in quotations, titles of books and articles, and names. The term "Bohemian", meaning unconventional, is derived from the French *bohéme*.

[2] Franz von Lutzow's *Bohemia*, p. 8; Ales Hrdlicka's *What Are the Czechoslovaks*, p. 22.

[3] Thomas Capek's *The Cechs in America*, pp. 3, 9-13.

Austrian and Czech newspapers as early as February, 1849. The "gold rush" to California affected Bohemia more than the other states of Austria and, during this period, twenty-five thousand Czechs emigrated to the United States. Local misfortunes such as floods or droughts and the consequent failures of potato crops also caused some of the Czechs to seek new homes.[4]

A more important economic reason for Czech emigration was the increasing desire of the farmers of Bohemia for more land. Until 1848 they had lived in a state of semi-serfdom. Austrian lords, who occupied the most valuable land, left for the Czech peasants individual holdings of approximately thirty-five to forty-two acres of undesirable land. After 1848, when serfdom was abolished in Austria and Hungary, many of these peasants gradually paid their redemption fees, sold their possessions, and migrated to the United States where land was cheap. Industrial opportunities in the United States also caused many of them to seek work here, because wages were higher than in Bohemia.[5]

Political causes for Czech emigration center about the Revolution of 1848. The bombardment of Prague on June 11, 1848, placed Bohemia under the absolute power of the Habsburgs and intensified the discontent of the Czechs. Many of the patriots, especially among the students, sought refuge in the United States. Some of the Czechs came to the United States to escape compulsory military service in the wars with Italy and Prussia, although this motive is likely to be exaggerated.[6]

---

[4] Capek's *The Cechs in America*, pp. 9, 28-33.

[5] Emily G. Balch's *The Peasant Background of Our Slavic Fellow Citizens* in *The Survey*, Vol. XXIV, pp. 668-678; Emily G. Balch's *Our Slavic Fellow Citizens*, p. 50.

[6] Lutzow's *Bohemia*, pp. 332-340; Josefa Humpal-Zeman's *Bohemian Settlements in the United States*, Industrial Commission *Reports*, Vol. XV, p. 507; Balch's *The Peasant Background of Our Slavic Fellow Citizens* in *The Survey*, Vol. XXIV, p. 674.

Data in regard to the number of Czechs in the United States are difficult to secure. The United States Census Reports do not deal with the question of nationality before 1910; until that date figures refer only to the countries from which immigrants are drawn. Bohemia is first named as the native country of foreign-born Czechs in the United States in the census of 1870.

Czech Population in the United States, Iowa, and Linn County[7]

Year	Country of Birth	Number in the United States	Number in Iowa	Number in Linn County
1870	Bohemia	40,289	6,766	1,780
1880	Bohemia	85,361	10,554	2,166
1890	Bohemia	118,106	10,928	3,327
1900	Bohemia	156,999	10,809	3,198
1920	Czechoslovakia	362,438	9,150	3,638
1930	Czechoslovakia	491,638	8,280	3,012

It may be observed from these statistics for Iowa that the greatest number of persons reported Bohemia as their birthplace in the year 1890. It may also be noted from the data for the United States that from 1870 to 1930 there was a constant increase in the number who indicated that Bohemia or Czechoslovakia had been their birthplace. The greatest increase was from 1920 to 1930. Political unrest among the Slovaks caused many of them to emigrate to the United States in the early 1920s.[8]

[7] Compiled from the Ninth, Tenth, Eleventh, Twelfth, and Fifteenth United States Census Reports. In 1910 the Thirteenth Census did not include Bohemia in the list of countries named as the birthplaces of foreign-born persons.

[8] Sarka B. Hrbkova's *Americans of Czecho-Slovak Descent* in *The Survey*, Vol. XLVI, pp. 361-368.

16

There are no statistical reports giving the exact number of persons of Czech descent who now live in Cedar Rapids, but it is estimated that about one-fourth of the city's population has Czech ancestry and that Cedar Rapids has the largest percentage of Czechs of any city in the United States.[9]

Czech Settlement in Cedar Rapids

The exact date for the first settlement of the Czechs in Iowa is not known. It is generally agreed, however, that they came to the banks of the Iowa River in Johnson County about 1850. Some of these pioneers soon pushed northward to better and more convenient locations along the banks of rivers and streams in College and Putnam townships in Linn County.[10]

Many of the first Czech immigrants came to Iowa from Racine or Caledonia, Wisconsin, by ox team. Others traveled to the Mississippi River by railroad and from there, by ferry and ox team, reached Johnson and Linn counties.[11] At that time, there were no railroads in Iowa. A military road, laid out in 1839, connected Dubuque with Iowa City. Most of the streams were bridged and travelers who wished "to view the country pretty generally, before locating, were asked to follow this road."[12] It is quite probable that early Iowa Czechs traveled along this road to Johnson County.

[9] Francis James Brown and J.S. Roucek's *Our Racial and National Minorities*, p. 233.
[10] J. Rudis Jicinsky's "Bohemians in Linn County, Iowa" in the *Atlas of Linn County*, p. 209.
[11] Joseph Mekota's "The Bohemian Element in the County" in Luther A. Brewer and Barthinius L. Wick's *History of Linn County, Iowa*, Vol. I, pp. 122-126.
[12] L.F. Andrew's "First Things in Iowa" in *Annals of Iowa* (Third Series), Vol. II, p. 394; Jacob Van der Zee's "Roads and Highways in Territorial Iowa" in *The Iowa Journal of History and Politics*, Vol. III, p. 222.

Thomas Korab, who came to Iowa with his parents in 1856, has written the following account of their journey to that state:

"My dear parents came from Moravia near Policka.... I remember very clearly, although I was only seven, our trip to America.... We came through Hamburg.

"The trip took twelve weeks. It was a stormy voyage and it made an impression, not only on me, but upon my parents. When we finally arrived in New York my father saluted the boat in tribute to it for bringing us safely here. We arrived at the Lorences, who lived in Racine, Wisconsin...in November, 1854. They were harvesting the corn. We could go no further because it was too late in the year. We lived in a log cabin; three families lived there. My father cut wood in the forest. As soon as spring arrived, my uncle came, by foot, to act as our guide from Wisconsin to Iowa. We bought a wagon and oxen and departed. The trip took two weeks. With us, in two other wagons, also came the Dostals and Lorences. It was the latter part of April, there was no grass, roads were bad, and it was very frosty. While the others went on, I was sent to one farm to buy something to eat and I got a loaf of bread fresh from the oven.... My uncle had a gun and whenever he saw a rabbit, he shot it. After a while, we finally came to the Lorences and Zvaceks, east of Ely [in Linn County]."[13]

Because many of these early pioneers were farmers, they did not come directly to Cedar Rapids, but instead purchased land south and southeast of the town. This they secured at a nominal price. For example, a deed, dated April 8, 1854, which is in the possession of Anna and Mary Woitishek, records that their grandfather, Vaclav Riegl, purchased twenty

[13] Thomas Korab's "Paměti českých osadníku v Americe" in *Amerikán Národní Kalendář*, 1925, p. 297.

acres of land in Linn County for one hundred dollars. Still cheaper was a farm of eighty acres in Section 29 of Linn County which Thomas Korab bought on April 4, 1862, for four dollars per acre. That land today is valued at about two hundred and fifty dollars an acre.[14]

After the purchase of a farm, the next task of the pioneer families was to erect a house. Often while clearing their land and preparing materials for the construction of a house, they lived with Czech families already established in the neighborhood. It was not uncommon for three families to live in a one-room log cabin. Sometimes sod houses were erected. Generally, however, because of the ample supply of timber, houses were constructed of logs. Both thatched and shingle roofs were used. Shingles, which were about four feet long, were cut by hand and were held in place on the roofs by logs placed across them.[15] Furniture for these early homes was scarce. Beds consisted of bundles of straw placed on the floor, on top of which were featherbeds brought from Bohemia in huge chests.

After the houses were constructed, land was cleared for crops. Where brush was cut away, beets were planted and where stumps were cleared, potatoes were planted. One pioneer recalls that, just after the Civil War, potatoes were sold for twenty-five cents a bag (about one and one-half bushels). Another farmer states that soon after 1858 he sold a load of potatoes in Cedar Rapids for ten cents a bushel. In 1870, Mr. Korab sold a load of straw for one dollar and twenty-five cents; corn for sixteen to eighteen cents a bushel; and hay for four to five dollars a ton.[16]

---

[14] Korab's "Paměti českých osadníku v Americe" in *Amerikán Národní Kalendář*, 1925, p. 298.

[15] Korab's "Paměti českých osadníku v Americe" in *Amerikán Národní Kalendář*, 1925, p. 298.

[16] A. Klobass' "Paměti českých osadníku v Americe" in *Amerikán Národní Kalendář*, 1915, pp. 245, 246; Korab's "Paměti českých osadníku v Americe" in *Amerikán Národní Kalendář*, 1925, p. 300.

When the young people of these pioneer families were not needed at home to help with the work, they sought employment elsewhere. Girls often became maids in Cedar Rapids homes.[17] One, for example, whose father was a farmer was sent to do housework so that she might learn the English language and thus help her father sell his produce. Another, whose family had been wealthy in Bohemia but whose funds were exhausted because of a poor investment, became a maid in the home of Judge George Greene. Unaccustomed to work of this type, she found housework an arduous task. During the Civil War, one boy worked for a farmer for fourteen dollars a month in the summer and nine dollars a month in the winter. Another, who was a tailor, went to Amana to work for twenty-two cents a day.[18]

When the Czechs first came to Cedar Rapids about 1852, they found a community with a population of less than four hundred people. In 1856, when the town charter was revised, there was a population of about 1500. The early Czech settlers built their homes on the east side of the Cedar River on South Third Street and from Fourth Street to Seventh Street south of Fourth Avenue. Early houses sometimes had but one or two rooms. Others are described as frame houses one story high.[19]

About nine years after the first Czechs settled in Cedar Rapids, the Civil War began. Living within the town, the population of which in 1860 was 1610, were about eighty Czech families. Seventeen of these Czechs, some of whom had left Bohemia to escape military service, volunteered to

[17] When harvest time came these girls sometimes returned to their homes to assist with the work.
[18] Balch's *Our Slavic Fellow Citizens*, p. 225; Korab's "Paměti českých osadníku v Americe" in *Amerikán Národní Kalendář*, 1925, p. 299; information concerning pioneer life was obtained from Mrs. Frank Krcmar, Mr. Wencil E. Wolrab, the Misses Anna and Mary Woitishek, and Mr. Milvoj Hasek, all children of pioneer families in Cedar Rapids.
[19] Luther A. Brewer and Barthinius L. Wick's *History of Linn County, Iowa*, Vol. I, pp. 334, 370; *The Cedar Rapids Times*, July 6, 1876.

serve their adopted country in the war. Frank Renchin, who had been a resident of Cedar Rapids for only seven years, was the first to enlist.[20]

That some of these volunteers were barely able to speak the English language is indicated by the incorrect spelling of their names in the *Roster and Record of Iowa Soldiers in the War of the Rebellion*. The youth of some of the Cedar Rapids Czechs who fought in the Civil War may also be noted: one was seventeen years old, five were eighteen, and two were nineteen. None was killed in battle; Frank Woitishek, however, died of disease at Vicksburg on July 18, 1863.

Following the Civil War, the Czech population of Cedar Rapids increased rapidly. Pioneers who had come in the 1850s wrote letters to their friends and relatives urging them to come to the United States and Cedar Rapids. Czech newspapers in the United States often announced good locations for the establishment of homes. *Slavie*, a paper published in Racine, printed letters of pioneers for the purpose of attracting others to certain localities. Likewise, colonization clubs in cities, such as Chicago, organized committees to search for habitable land for Czech immigrants.[21]

Shipping companies and railroads vied with each other in bidding for the patronage of foreigners. For example, Carpenter, Stibbs and Company, agents for the "Anchor Line"

---

[20] Sarka B. Hrbkova's "Bohemians Have Done Much for Cedar Rapids" in *The Cedar Rapids Republican Semi-Centennial Magazine Edition*, June 10, 1906. Those who enlisted were: Frank Dolleshel (Dolezal), Frank Wortershak (Woitishek), Wentzel Dolleshel (Dolezal), Frank Renchin, Enos Watrobek (Vatroubek), John Watrobek (Vatroubek), Wentzel Banish (Benes), Jacob Cherny (Cerny), Frantisek Horak, Joseph Liposky, Joseph Podhasky, John Ratzek, Anthony Sulek, Frank Peremsky (Premsky), John Wedra (Vydra), Wenzel Watroubek (Vatroubek), and Joseph Bednar. – *Roster and Record of Iowa Soldiers in the War of the Rebellion*, Vols. II, III, IV, V.

[21] Mekota's "The Bohemian Element in the County" in Brewer and Wick's *History of Linn County, Iowa*, Vol. I, p. 123; Rosicky's *A History of the Czechs in Nebraska*, p. 26.

of weekly steamers, advertised that they were prepared to issue through tickets from European ports, including Hamburg and Bremen, to Cedar Rapids. Also persons "desiring to send for their friends in Europe or to remit money to them" would be accommodated at the local office with tickets or foreign drafts.[22]

Immigration to Iowa was also stimulated by the work of the state immigration agencies. From 1860 to 1862 Iowa had its first Commissioner of Immigration who maintained an office in New York. There he made contacts with new immigrants and published descriptions of Iowa in foreign newspapers. From 1870 to 1873 a State Board of Immigration not only published handbooks in several foreign languages, but sent agents to European ports to persuade foreigners to locate in Iowa. The state spent a total of $29,500 to encourage immigration.[23]

That the efforts of these various agencies increased immigration is evident from a brief news item which appeared in a Cedar Rapids newspaper early in May, 1868. The reporter commented that "the number of accessions by immigration to the population of Linn County this spring" was larger than he had ever known it since his residence in the community. A news report three weeks later spoke of "the increased influx of strangers into Cedar Rapids."[24]

Because a large majority of these Czech immigrants came to the United States for economic reasons, it is important to observe their occupational interests in Cedar Rapids. One of the first of the Czechs to establish a business (in partnership with a Mr. Fort) was Jerome Vostrovsky who lived in Cedar Rapids from 1867 to 1871. In October, 1867, a full column appeared in a local newspaper advertising the firm of Fort and Vostrovsky which made "a specialty of Dress Goods, Ladies'

---

[22] Advertisement in *The Cedar Valley Times*, April 2, 1868.
[23] Marcus L. Hansen's "Official Encouragement of Immigration to Iowa" in *The Iowa Journal of History and Politics*, Vol. XIX, pp. 159-195.
[24] *The Cedar Valley Times*, May 7, 28, 1868.

Furnishings Goods, Gloves, Hosiery, Hoop-Skirts, Balmoral Skirts of every description, Shawls, etc., etc.,...[and sold] no Shoddy Goods at any price."[25]

The earliest available source from which to obtain information in regard to the occupations of the Czechs is a Cedar Rapids *Directory* published in 1870. It lists 128 people of Czech descent most of whom were undoubtedly heads of families. It gives the occupations of these people as follows: laborers, 23; shoemakers, 20, including one listed as an apprentice; blacksmiths, 8; clerks, 8; tailors, 5; wagon makers, 6; salesmen, 4; tinners, 3; collar makers, 3; saloon keepers, 3; cigar makers, 2; grocers, 2; harness makers, 2; teamsters, 2; and bookkeepers, 2. In addition, one person only is listed for each of the following occupations: machinist, dry goods merchant, cabinet maker, butcher, teacher, lawyer, manager of billiard hall, railroad man, hotel keeper, farmer, servant girl, mechanical engineer, carpenter, stone cutter, law student, and editor of the Czech newspaper, *Pokrok.*

Sometime previous to 1873 Frank Dvorak made "calf-skin boots with bronze morocco tops, high French heels, and glove-fitting fronts for $12 a pair." Thomas Capek quotes Frederick Jonas as saying that Joseph Sosel, who had located in Cedar Rapids in 1858, was undoubtedly the first Czech lawyer in the United States.[26]

The *Cedar Rapids Directory*, published in 1877, records a total of 3,089 people, 387 of whom were of Czech descent. Apparently most of the people listed were heads of households. In a section of this *Directory* which is devoted to brief accounts of prominent business people, several Czechs were mentioned. Among these are Wencil Janda whose specialty was "fine, scenic, fresco, and ornamental painting;"

[25] Rosicky's *A History of the Czechs in Nebraska*, p. 50; *The Cedar Valley Times*, November 28, 1867.
[26] *Cedar Rapids City Directory*, 1870-1871; Charles A. Laurance's *Pioneer Days in Cedar Rapids*, p. 55; Capek's *The Cechs in America*, p. 85. Joseph Sosel had an unusually interesting career.

Frank Horak, who kept a full stock of groceries and conducted a boarding house having fourteen rooms; Frank Dvorak, who, in addition to being a shoemaker, was also the conductor of the Cedar Rapids Light Guard Band; and John Petrovitsky who had "a nice meat market" where he manufactured sausage casings and "gave employment to twenty hands."[27]

At the same time that the Czech people of Cedar Rapids were developing their economic interests, they were also enjoying social activities. Dances were held on Saturday nights in the Bohemian Dance Hall.[28] Judging from several newspaper accounts, these dances sometimes terminated on "Sabbath morning...in a first-class-rough-and-tumble-set-to." "Why do not our city Fathers", bewails a reporter in 1868, "take the necessary steps to get this interesting territory inside the corporation? It would certainly be a great acquisition to our city, as that dance hall is one of the institutions of the country."[29]

Two months later, the newspaper again complained about the "disgraceful scenes which were perpetrated" in the dance hall. This time, however, the reporter commented:

> "We do not wish to be understood as laying all the disgraceful occurrences in that vicinity to our Bohemian citizens; on the contrary, we are informed...that all or nearly all the disturbance is caused by Americans, young men of the 'manor born', who visit this house solely for the purpose of raising a disturbance with the Bohemians, and generally succeed in so doing, making causes for disturbing them, when if let alone to enjoy themselves in their own way, there would be no trouble."[30]

---

[27] *Cedar Rapids Directory*, 1877-1878.
[28] The exact location of this hall is not known, but it was probably on Third Street Southeast.
[29] *The Cedar Valley Times*, May 7, 1868.
[30] *The Cedar Valley Times*, July 2, 1868.

24

After about 1875 no statement of trouble at the dances appears in the papers. Either the Americans ceased to attend the Czech functions or the newspapers failed to take cognizance of disorderly events. Previous to 1875, reporters may have regarded the Czechs as undesirable foreigners and for that reason they may have overemphasized the disturbances at the dances.

As early as 1870, July 6th was observed as Jan Hus Day in commemoration of the burning of their national hero in 1415. Milvoj Hasek recalls that, from about 1875 to 1880, the Czech people would congregate in the evening in a grove on the west side of the river south of Sixteenth Avenue. There a huge bonfire would be kindled and around it the Czechs would assemble to sing their national songs and listen to short speeches.

The Fourth of July was also celebrated with picnics and parades. In 1877, a typical parade was described as follows:

"The procession was formed in the city, and was as fine a display as has graced our streets in many a day. About one hundred little girls, dressed in white and neatly decorated with red and blue ribbons was a most pleasing feature, and one which we have never seen surpassed in a procession of this kind. Headed by the Bohemian Brass Band they marched to the grove at the end of Park Avenue [Third Avenue] where speeches, music, and a good social time generally were enjoyed.... To our Bohemian citizens belongs the honor of doing appropriate and full honors to that natal day of their country."[31]

The following year Independence Day was observed with a more elaborate procession. Young ladies carried the flag and a "bouquet-decorated" standard. They were followed by "children, young men, the Bohemian band...a long line of

[31] *The Cedar Rapids Times*, July 5, 1877.

Bohemian Citizens," the Sokols in full uniform, and the Reading Society. "It is a source of genuine pleasure and an assurance of safety in the future," observes the reporter, "to see our foreign-born citizens celebrate the anniversary of American Independence."[32]

To the Czech women a "dračky" (a feather-stripping party) was a source of pleasure and a means of securing down for featherbeds and pillows. In preparation for it, feathers were stripped from fowls, preferably geese and ducks, in the late fall. These feathers were then dried and tied in bags. During the winter, groups of women met in each other's homes for a "dračky". They sat about a table on which were two large inverted bowls. Feathers kept under one were removed single and stripped of down which was then placed under the other bowl. Sometimes the party lasted all day and into the evening. In the afternoon coffee and kolaches[33] were served. Feather-stripping parties are still a part of the social life of some of the Czech women in Cedar Rapids.[34]

A considerable number of the Czechs who settled in the community before 1880 were craftsmen, but after that year the number of laborers who made Cedar Rapids their home tended to increase. Economic changes in Bohemia were partially responsible for this change. In addition, between 1870 and 1880, opportunities for laborers to find employment in Cedar Rapids were increased by the erection of two new factories.[35]

That the number of Czech laborers was increasing is established by comparing the occupations of these people as they are listed in the directories of 1870, 1877, and 1881. In

---

[32] *The Cedar Rapids Times*, July 11, 1878.
[33] Kolaches (koláče) are sweet rolls filled with fruit, poppy seed, or Dutch cheese mixed with sugar and egg.
[34] Information concerning a "dračky" was furnished by Mrs. Joseph Kralik and Mrs. F.J. Krcmar.
[35] The T.M. Sinclair and Company Meat Packing Plant was built in 1871. The factory of Stuart and Douglas, manufacturers of oatmeal and pearl barley, was built in 1874.

the *Directory* for 1870, 113 Czechs who were gainfully employed were listed; of these 23 persons or 20.3 per cent of the total were designated as laborers. The *Directory* for 1877 recorded 263 Czechs who were employed and of these, 77 or 29.2 per cent were listed as laborers. In the *Directory* for 1881, 385 Czechs were listed and of these, 147 or 38.1 per cent were recorded as laborers. That some of the occupations of the people were requiring less skill is also shown by the fact that in 1877 there were fifteen carpenters and seven cabinet makers listed in the *Directory*; in the 1881 *Directory* there were twenty carpenters and only one cabinet maker.[36]

Evidence of the increasing business ability of the Czechs during the 1880s is found in the account of an Independence Day parade in 1889. Nine of the sixty-five industrial floats in the parade advertised Czech firms of three hardware merchants, two harness makers, two grocers, one brick mason, and one tailor. C.H. Swab and Company had "a complete outfit of tinners at work making stove pipes, tin cups, and other articles. The tin cups were distributed by liberal hands among the crowd." The float of J. Vosmek and Company, which was one of the three in the whole parade to tie for first prize, "was a large room made of canvass decorated with the national colors and inscriptions. Inside were thirteen tailors actually at work."

This parade not only represented some of the economic activities of the Czechs in 1889, but it also indicated the participation of these people in local civic affairs. In 1877 and 1878 the Czech people had observed July Fourth with their own parades; in 1889 they shared in one which represented all of the citizens of Cedar Rapids.[37]

Another phase of the participation of the Czechs in municipal affairs is their election or appointment to public offices. Frank Witousek, who was elected alderman in 1877

---

[36] *Cedar Rapids City Directory*, 1870-1871, 1877-1878, 1881-1882.
[37] *The Cedar Rapids Times*, July 11, 1889.

and 1878, was the first Czech in Cedar Rapids to hold an office and Frank Kouba, alderman in 1883 and 1884, was the second office holder. Since 1883 there has never been a year in which Czech people have not held one or more elective or appointive positions in the city. The length of time which some of the individual Czechs have held local offices is noticeable. Louis J. Zika, for example, who was Commissioner of Public Improvement from 1910 to 1926 and from 1928 until his death, April 13, 1934, held an elective municipal office the longest of any single individual in the history of Cedar Rapids. Other Czech citizens who have held local positions for a considerable number of years and longer than anyone else in the respective positions to which they have been appointed include: Vaclav E. Vane, auditor for thirty-two years; Anton Tlusty, health officer for twenty-six years and assistant health officer for twelve years; Vaclav Janda, sidewalk inspector for fourteen years and street commissioner for sixteen years; and Frank Barta, sewer inspector for forty-three years. Of the twenty-two different men elected to the city council between 1918 and 1943, six have belonged to the Czech group.[38]

Throughout their settlement in Cedar Rapids, it has been the ambition of a large majority of the Czech people to own their own homes. The Bohemian Savings and Loan Association has greatly aided them in the acquisition of property and erection of houses. Plans for this organization were first discussed in a meeting of the Reading Society in 1885 when Jan V. Kouba presented the by-laws of a Czech Building and Loan Club in Chicago. Those present decided that it was inadvisable to start a similar organization in Cedar Rapids, but on December 13, 1891, a small group met in the Reading Society Hall, chose temporary officers, and planned for a mass meeting on December 26th. For the first six months

---

[38] William H. Stepanek's *History of the Municipal Affairs of Cedar Rapids, Iowa*, 1936, pp. 49-52. Information was also obtained from reports furnished by the Cedar Rapids Chamber of Commerce.

of the organization, all officers and directors, except the secretary, served without pay. The latter's salary during that time was two dollars a week.[39]

The total assets of the organization at the first meeting amounted to $129.75. When the Czech (Bohemian) Savings and Loan Association observed its fiftieth anniversary on January 2, 1942, its assets were $1,661,534.20. Years of generous service on the part of some of the officers of the association largely account for its progress. Jan J. Hrbek, for example, was a director from January 8, 1893, until his death in 1943, and Joseph Urban has served as director and treasurer since January 15, 1905. John V. Rompotl, the present secretary, estimates that about 75 per cent of the Czech people in Cedar Rapids now own their own homes and that a majority of these people pay up their loans in five years instead of the eleven years specified in the contract.[40]

Five years after the founding of the Bohemian Savings and Loan Association, a group of Czechs, headed again by Jan V. Kouba, organized the Bohemian Mutual Insurance Society to insure their property against fire and lightning. This association provided for the insurance of commercial buildings for one year at a time and houses, furniture, and household equipment for five years, all for 75 per cent of their actual value if within the limits of Cedar Rapids and in areas to which city water was piped, but otherwise for only 50 per cent of their value. No policy for more than $1800 could be carried on any one piece of property.[41]

---

[39] Jan J. Hrbek's "*České spolky vypomocný a pojistující*" in *Památník česko-amerického dne při zlatém jubileu města Cedar Rapids, 14 června, 1906*, pp. 25, 26.

[40] *The Cedar Rapids Gazette*, January 3, 1942; information obtained from John V. Rompotl.

[41] Vaclav Janda's "*České spolky vypomocný a pojistující*" in *Památník česko-amerického dne při zlatém jubileu města Cedar Rapids, 14 června, 1906*, p. 26.

Houses which the Czech people have erected largely through the financial aid and protection of these two organizations are located, for the most part, in the extreme southeast and southwest sections of the city. Because these people are practical and frugal, they have not only built houses which are modest and neat, but they have kept their homes in excellent repair. Yards are filled with shade trees, fruit trees, and shrubs, and gardens are beautiful with flowers.

Because so many of the Czech people began to build their homes, after 1900, in the southwest section of the city, Czech businessmen also commenced to erect their shops on the west side of the river. The *Directory* for 1870 shows that Commercial Street (First Street) was the chief business street for the Czechs, as well as others, at that time. By 1881 the *Directory* indicates a shift of many Czech business concerns to Third Street SE. In 1906 Louis J. Pochobradsky built a grocery store on Sixteenth Avenue near C Street SW. He was followed, in 1908, by Frank J. John[42] who opened a harness shop in a small frame building on the south side of the avenue. Later he built the first brick structure in the vicinity, across the avenue from his first location. Nearby, John N. Kucera erected a hardware store and Frank Muzik opened a cigar manufacturing shop. Gradually other Czech businessmen moved to Sixteenth Avenue. Today, with its two and one-half blocks of stores owned almost entirely by Czechs, that avenue is the chief commercial district of the Czechs in Cedar Rapids.

One of the activities of some of the Czech men whose homes were in the southeast section of the city was service in the Third Ward Volunteer Fire Company. The hose house was located on Third Street between Ninth and Tenth avenues. This fire company was the first one in the city to acquire uniforms gay with bright red shirts and red helmets. Dances had been held for months in the Reading Society Hall in order

---

[42] Frank J. John (Jan) is one of the few Czechs in Cedar Rapids who has Anglicized the spelling of his name.

to secure funds with which to purchase these uniforms. Because the firemen of the Czech unit were proud of their accomplishment, they sent their picture to the Náprstek Museum in Prague.[43]

Two outstanding occasions for the Czech people in Cedar Rapids between 1900 and 1910 were their participation in the semi-centennial celebration in 1906 commemorating the founding of Cedar Rapids and a lecture by Thomas G. Masaryk. Both reveal the attitude of the Czech people toward their adopted country. Bohemian Day, observed on June 14, 1906, during the semi-centennial week, summarized many of the achievements of the Czech people during fifty years of residence in Cedar Rapids. At ten o'clock in the morning they assembled in Riverside Park to dedicate a boulder bearing this inscription: "1856 Česko-Americký Den, 14. Června, 1906. Semi-Centennial, Cedar Rapids, Iowa." Kouba's band played and Joseph Mekota concluded a speech with the statement that "Cedar Rapids is known as the Bohemian Athens of America."

At one o'clock that day there was a street parade over six blocks long participated in by the Sokols, the school children, hundreds of men in full uniform from the various lodges, members of the ladies' societies in hacks, and farmers on horseback. This part of the parade was followed by four allegorical floats designed by Irma Rudis and J. Kosar, a Chicago artist. One of these bore the title, "Homage of the Bohemians to Cedar Rapids." A woman who symbolized Cedar Rapids sat on a throne surrounded by four other women who represented art, science, labor, and manufacturing. Facing her, Czech settlers offered her small replicas of the CSPS Hall, the Catholic Church, and the Czech School. A Sokol, who stood at one side surrounded by a few of his pupils holding aloft an American flag, presented a wreath to Cedar

---

[43] This information was furnished by Milvoj Hasek. The Náprstek Museum was founded by Vojta Náprstek, a former Czech exile to the United States.

Rapids. A blacksmith who symbolized labor offered her a horseshoe. Following the parade, a grand festival was held in Riverside Park where booths were arranged in "old country" fashion. There was music by the Czech bands, singing by the Czech school children, drills by the Sokols, the lodges, and the Catholic societies, and speeches by Mayor Connor, Professor Bohumil Shimek of the State University of Iowa, Father Florian Svrdlik, and L.J. Palda.[44]

The lecture by Thomas G. Masaryk on September 13, 1907, was given at the Czech School. To a large crowd, honored to hear a man well known among his countrymen even at that time, he spoke of the existing differences between the schools of Bohemia and the United States. His concluding advice to his listeners was:

> "You who come to America should first of all learn to speak the English language.... But while you should work indefatigably for the advancement and good of the community in which you live, you need not therefore abandon your Bohemian traditions and your interest in Bohemian history and institutions.... However, a live, earnest, and sincere share of your efforts should be directed to being worthy citizens of this United States."[45]

The most important business activities of the Czechs in 1941 and the number who were owners of their own establishments were: grocers, 28; tavern keepers, 22; owners of meat markets, 22; contractors, 14; shoe repair men, 12; filling station operators, 11; druggists, 9; painters and decorators, 9; barbers, 7; bakers, 6; automobile repair men, 6; real estate agents, 6; and tailors, 6. While there were by no means as many tailors in the city in 1941 as there had been in

---

[44] *The Cedar Rapids Republican*, June 15, 1906.
[45] *The Cedar Rapids Republican*, September 14, 1907.

32

1880, still 50 per cent of all the people engaged in that handicraft in 1941 were Czechs.[46]

The entrance of people of this lineage into professions in which they were scarcely represented in 1880 is noticeable in 1941. In 1880, for example, there were two Czech lawyers; in 1941 there were thirteen. In 1880 there were no Czech dentists; in 1941 there were sixteen. Also in 1880 there were no Czech physicians; in 1941 there were eighteen. The percentage of Czech people represented in some of the professions in 1941 is of interest. For example, 10 per cent of all the lawyers in the city, 22.2 per cent of the dentists, and 20.2 per cent of the physicians and surgeons were Czechs. The *Directory* lists five Czech graduate nurses and seven clergymen but not any teachers of that nationality, although it is known that some of the public school teachers were of Czech descent. Thus by 1941 the Czechs had entered practically all of the businesses and professions in Cedar Rapids. In 1938 a Distinguished Service Award was presented to Ervin Stepanek.[47]

---

[46] *Cedar Rapids City Directory*, 1941, pp. 583 ff.
[47] *Cedar Rapids City Directory*, 1941. This award is presented annually by the Young Men's Bureau of the Chamber of Commerce to not more than two men not over thirty-five years of age for outstanding civic work. See Reports of the Cedar Rapids Chamber of Commerce.

Cultural Organizations of the Czechs

"One of the most surprising facts in the life of the Slavs in America", says Emily G. Balch, "is the degree to which they are organized into societies."[48] There appears to be nothing in their European background which accounts for the formation of these numerous organizations, but when Czechs, who were imbued with a natural love for music, dramatics, and dancing, settled in groups where all spoke the same language and had similar characteristics and like interests, formal organizations soon developed around their common interests.

Čtenářský Spolek (The Reading Society)

The Čtenářský Spolek was the first organization of the Czech people in Cedar Rapids. Joseph Kohout and Frank Renchin summoned the Czechs of the community to a meeting in Concert Hall, First Avenue and First Street NE, on November 8, 1868. A discussion ensued concerning the type of organization which was deemed most desirable. Some wanted a loan society and others a dramatic club. A motion in favor of the latter was carried by a majority vote.[49]

A second meeting was summoned for the purpose of choosing a definite name for the society. Jaroslav Vostrovsky presented the name *"Slavie"* (Glory); Vaclav Dolezal suggested *"Slovanská Lípa"* (Slavic Linden); and John Vydra proposed *"Čtenářský Spolek"* (Reading Society). The last name was adopted by a majority vote of the forty-one charter members. As adopted at a regular meeting on November 22, 1868, the by-laws stated that the purpose of the organization was to encourage reading, to promote lectures, and to present

[48] Balch's *Our Slavic Fellow Citizens*, p. 378.
[49] Minutes of the Čtenářský Spolek for November 8, 1868.

dramatic performances for "universal education and entertainment". They also provided that all men and "any lady who is sixteen and who enjoys a blameless reputation may become a member of the society." The women did not take advantage of this opportunity, however, and the provision was later dropped.[50]

The first entertainment of the Reading Society was presented on December 28, 1868. Unfortunately the minutes do not state the exact nature of this program except to record that two men and three ladies gave orations, that the wives of the members furnished refreshments, and that $291.48 was collected, of which $225 was profit. Twenty-five dollars of this amount was immediately appropriated for the purchase of books from "*Slavie*", a publishing company in Racine, Wisconsin.[51]

For the year 1869 several important events of a miscellaneous nature are recorded in the minutes. During the year fifty-two new members joined the organization which, with the aid of Josef Sosel, was incorporated. In April a play entitled "Dobré jitro" (Good Morning) was presented in Brown's Hall.[52] An interesting detail in the minutes states that actors were allowed five dollars for refreshments during the rehearsals of the plays. A brief account in a local newspaper concerning this first play says that "our reporter was present and pronounced that the entertainment in every respect was creditable."[53]

The most important business of the year was the formulation of plans for the construction of a permanent hall. A lot was purchased on Commercial Street and Green Avenue (First Street and Fifth Avenue) for one thousand dollars. On

---

[50] L.J. Palda's *Sin čtenářského spolku v Cedar Rapids, Iowa*, in *Květy Americké*, Vol. III, p. 160.
[51] Minutes of the Čtenářský Spolek for December 28, 1868.
[52] Brown's Hall was the third floor of a building on First Street near First Avenue NE.
[53] *The Marion Register*, April 14, 1869.

December 5th a method for financing the erection of the hall was adopted which was both unique and also indicative of a lack of wealth among the members. It provided for the issuance of five-dollar bonds to mature in three years at 10 per cent interest. Each three months thereafter these bonds were to be paid off according to numbers drawn by lot.[54]

Both the minutes of the organization and a newspaper account describe the dedication of the Reading Society Hall. In the afternoon of June 6, 1870, the members of the society and several hundred other Czechs, including some from nearby towns, met at Brown's Hall and marched in a parade to the new hall. Headed by the younger school children, there followed the Bohemian Brass Band, four little girls dressed in white carrying a wreath, and the older school children "two of whom carried the Bohemian and American flags flying side by side." The parade stopped in front of the new hall where the contractor presented the keys of the building to the president, Josef Hrbek. Speeches were then given by Mr. Hrbek, Mr. Zdrubek, and Mr. Sommer and "a declamation was rendered by five little girls." In the evening a comedy, "Pan Stryček" (Mr. Uncle), presented in the new building, concluded the dedicatory ceremonies.[55]

The Reading Society Hall was a one-story frame structure one hundred feet long and forty-two feet wide. The stage was twenty feet deep and was equipped with scenery which, according to the newspaper, was "chaste and appropriate". The assembly room was also used for a dance hall and the dressing rooms were located under the stage. The total cost of the structure was four thousand dollars. "It was not elegant," remarked a contemporary, "but it was ours."[56]

---

[54] Minutes of the Čtenářský Spolek for the year 1869.

[55] *The Cedar Rapids Times*, June 16, 1870; Anton Soukup's *"Čtenářský Spolek"* in *Památník česko-amerického dne při zlatém jubileu města Cedar Rapids, 14 června, 1906*, p. 33.

[56] *The Cedar Rapids Times*, June 16, 1870; Palda's *Sin čtenářského spolku v Cedar Rapids, Iowa*, in *Květy Americké*, Vol. III, p. 160.

36

A month later, on July 6, 1870, the Reading Society observed Jan Hus Day. In the afternoon fourteen wagons of farmers, who came to attend the program, were met at the bridge by the band and a group of girls in Czech costume, one of whom carried the Society's flag.[57] In the afternoon there were speeches and music. In the evening, the play "Jan Hus" was presented for the first time on any Czech stage in the United States. Aside from the fact that Frank Zbanek played the part of Jan Hus, descriptive details of the play are lacking.[58]

In the years which followed, the Reading Society served as a nucleus for several auxiliary organizations. An idea of its activities may be gained from an account of it which appears in the *Directory* for 1877. The public was admitted each Wednesday night to the gymnastic classes. The dramatic club of twenty-five members possessed "a very fine wardrobe". The gymnasium was equipped with six hundred dollars' worth of necessary apparatus. The library was supplied with five hundred volumes of well-chosen books.[59] In order to clear the debt of the organization as soon as possible, the hall was rented to groups for dances for fifteen dollars, and whenever a play was presented, all of the actors paid their own admissions.[60]

Several years later when all debts were paid, an addition to the hall was built to be used for a library. Besides supplying books for this library, the society and its auxiliary organizations continued to sponsor a variety of activities. Among these were the observance of the Battle of White Mountain and the birthdays of Jan Amos Komensky and

[57] The society still has this flag. It is made of silk with three wide stripes of red, white, and blue. In the center is the symbol of Bohemia, a two-tailed lion. Around this is the inscription, "Čtenářský Spolek".
[58] Soukup's "Čtenářský Spolek" in *Památník česko-amerického dne při zlatém jubileu města Cedar Rapids, 14 června, 1906*, p. 33; information obtained from Mrs. J.J. Hervert, daughter of Frank Zbanek.
[59] *The Cedar Rapids City Directory*, 1877-1878, p. 33.
[60] Soukup's "Čtenářský Spolek" in *Památník česko-amerického dne při zlatém jubileu města Cedar Rapids, 14 června, 1906*, p. 33.

Thomas Paine, the maintenance of a school with John B. Suster as the teacher, the rehearsals of a choral society with Vaclav Koubat as singing master, and the continuance of dramatic productions every two weeks under the direction of Josef Kohout, Sr., Frank B. Zdrubek, and John Vosmek. Gradually the auxiliary organizations broke away from the Reading Society and became independent units.[61]

After the construction of the Prokop Velký Hall in 1891, the hall of the Reading Society was no longer a popular place for social activities. Moreover the commercial interests of the city had moved into the vicinity of the hall and the location was no longer desirable. Hence the property was sold to Faye Brothers Lumber Company and meetings of the society were held temporarily in the Sokol Hall. With the erection of the Matice Školská (Czech School) in 1900, the organization had rooms on the second floor of this building for its meetings and for its library.[62] The chief function of the organization today is to maintain this library, but meetings are still held consisting of educational and recreational features. Women were admitted to membership in 1938. The young people manifest little interest in the organization and scarcely ever attend its meetings, but between forty and fifty adults enthusiastically support the activities of the Čtenářský Spolek.[63]

---

[61] Hrbkova's "Bohemians Have Done Much for Cedar Rapids" in *The Cedar Rapids Republican Semi-Centennial Magazine Edition*, June 10, 1906.

[62] Soukup's "Čtenářský Spolek" in *Památník česko-amerického dne při zlatém jubileu města Cedar Rapids, 14 června, 1906*, p. 34.

[63] This information was furnished by Josef Holub, one of the present librarians of the society.

38

Musical Activities

The inherent love of the Czech people for music has been expressed in the formation of their numerous musical organizations. To these people in Cedar Rapids bands have seemed to be an absolute necessity. These musical organizations have not only been indispensable for all of the parades, funeral processions, programs, plays, dedications of buildings, and the festivals of the Czech people, but they have supplied the whole city with a popular type of music.

The first band in Cedar Rapids, known as the Light Guard Band, which was organized in 1869 or 1870, probably made its first appearance at the dedication of the Reading Society Hall. This first musical organization with eleven members met with little success in its early days because the members of it spoke only the Czech language, but later gained fame when Frank Dvorak, who understood the English language, became its efficient manager and Vaclav Charipar became its leader.[64]

In 1872, Frank Kouba, who was a very good musician, came to Cedar Rapids and immediately organized a band of young men. It was called by several names: Kouba's National Band, The National Cornet Band and Orchestra, and The Bohemian Brass Band. At first it supplied music only for dances, then more members were added, uniforms were secured, and before long it gained a state-wide reputation. During the thirty-four years of its existence, this group of musicians played not only in Cedar Rapids but in nearby

---

[64] Hrbkova's "Bohemians Have Done Much for Cedar Rapids" in the *Cedar Rapids Republican Semi-Centennial Magazine Edition*, June 10, 1906; Boleslav Jandera's "Hudba česká v Cedar Rapids" in *Památník česko-amerického dne při zlatém jubileu města Cedar Rapids, 14 června, 1906*, p. 27; information furnished by Joseph Sadowsky and Mrs. T.M. Thomas.

towns for parties, election rallies, plays, state fairs, firemen's tournaments, picnics, and parades for various occasions.[65]

Three other Czech bands deserve mention: Kubicek's Band, composed of fifteen men, which was organized in 1894, Mokrej's Band with a personnel of eighteen men which gained well deserved fame in 1896, and Jansa's Band organized in 1900, and at that time composed of ten young men all under twenty-one years of age. The leader, who had played in a military band in Bohemia, directed his organization with military precision. One of the former members of it recalls that Mr. Jansa often said: "Boys, the beginnings of pieces are important. Do your work willingly, be polite to your instructor, and see that no discord comes between you."[66]

The first Czech orchestra in Cedar Rapids, founded by Vaclav Koubat in 1870, gained notoriety because of the musical ability of its leader. He was known as the father of music among his own people and was often in demand for "parlor music" in Cedar Rapids homes because of his skill as a violinist. His orchestra of seven men furnished music of a high type both within the city and also in communities as far distant as one hundred miles from Cedar Rapids.

A second Czech orchestra of note was founded in 1875 by Professor Frank Pirkl. In addition to conducting this musical group, he gave lessons on the guitar, violin, and piano. He was known as "a thoroughly educated musician who was well qualified to teach." After his death in 1895, his son, Frank Pirkl, Jr., became the director of this organization. A third orchestra, which was considered one of the leading musical groups in the city, was directed by Josef Tlapa from about 1886 to 1902. At the same time he taught vocal and instrumental music and continued with his voice instruction even after he ceased to direct his orchestra in 1902. In the

---

[65] Jandera's "Hudba česká v Cedar Rapids" in *Památník česko-amerického dne při zlatém jubileu města Cedar Rapids, 14 června, 1906*, p. 27.
[66] Jandera's "Hudba česká v Cedar Rapids" in *Památník česko-amerického dne při zlatém jubileu města Cedar Rapids, 14 června, 1906*, p. 27.

other orchestras of Cedar Rapids which were not distinctly
Czech organizations, many of the musicians were people of
that nationality.[67]
    The Czech love of music also manifested itself in vocal
organizations. A choral club, founded in the winter of 1870,
was at first an auxiliary of the Reading Society. This group of
ten vocalists was later affiliated with the Thalee Society,
which in 1872 bought a lot and erected a hall at the west end
of Legare Street (Tenth Avenue) near the river. Five years
later this organization had a membership of eighty persons.[68]
    In 1873 a new choral society, known as the Lyra Club,
was organized under the direction of Frank Pirkl but a short
time later the Česká Beseda society superseded the Lyra Club.
The Hlahol Society, composed of nineteen men, was
organized on January 1, 1905. The director was Josef Tlapa
and the assistant director was K.F. Kirchner. Evidence of the
way in which various Czech organizations helped each other is
shown here by the fact that the Sokols loaned the new Hlahol
Society their hall for its rehearsals. The director and his
assistant wrote out the single voice parts so it was unnecessary
to buy music books. After several weeks a piano was
purchased from F.W. Slapnicka which was paid for by
voluntary contributions of ten and twenty dollars from the
individual members. By January 9, 1906, women were also
asked to join the society. During the years of its existence,
this choral organization sang for Czech Memorial Day
services, for plays, and for entertainments; presented operettas
at the CSPS Hall; and observed its tenth anniversary on
December 1, 1914, with the presentation of an especially fine

[67] *Cedar Rapids City Directory*, 1877-1878, p. 34; *Biographical Record of Linn County* (1901), p. 629; Jandera's "Hudba česká v Cedar Rapids" in *Památník česko-amerického dne při zlatém jubileu města Cedar Rapids, 14 června, 1906*, p. 28.
[68] *The Cedar Rapids City Directory*, 1877-1878, p. 33.

concert. Too many other attractions after 1918 finally caused the breakup of the Hlahol Society.[69]

While the Czech people promoted their own musical interests they also brought to the local community entertainments for themselves and the other citizens. An outstanding attraction was a concert presented on May 7, 1923, at the Majestic Theatre by the Bakule children. This was a chorus which had been formed at the Bakule school for crippled children in Prague which had been aided by the American Junior Red Cross. The chorus came to the United States under the auspices of President Masaryk and the Czechoslovak Red Cross "to express in the universal language of song the appreciation and sympathy" rendered Czech children by American children through the American Junior Red Cross whose guests they were in the United States.[70]

The next musical feature which many of the citizens of Cedar Rapids were privileged to hear was the Prague School Teachers' Chorus, which came in the fall of 1928. It presented a concert to a large audience at the Shrine Temple. The first part of the program consisted of classical selections by famous Czech composers and the last part was a group of the folk songs of Czechoslovakia. That the audience was especially appreciative of this part of the concert was evident when older Czech people wept and shouted to the chorus in their native tongue between the numbers of the program. In commenting on the concert a reporter said:

"It remained for the Prague School Teachers' Chorus to bring more closely into American hearts the music of the Czechs.... Musical critics of the country

[69] Karel F. Kirchner's "Pěvecký sbor Hlahol" in *Památník česko-amerického dne při zlatém jubileu města Cedar Rapids, 14 června, 1906*, p. 30; *The Cedar Rapids Republican*, October 25, 1914. Czech Memorial Day is the first Sunday in June. Services are then held at the Bohemian National Cemetery.

[70] *The Cedar Rapids Gazette*, May 8, 1923.

have pronounced them 'the greatest singing body in the world and the world's most perfect chorus'."[71]

In 1932 Frank Chramosta was responsible for the first Czech radio program broadcast by the local station WMT. During that year Ben Jansa and his band furnished instrumental music, joined by Mr. Chramosta and Miss Alice Spevacek in vocal duets. These programs continued for six years with music by various Czech bands, semi-weekly concerts by George Cervenka's orchestra, talks by Jaroslava Holubova concerning the interests of the Czech people, and vocal numbers by Wencil Andrle and Alice Spevacek. Beginning with March 3, 1940, broadcasts were sponsored by the Czech Alliance. Since then Sunday morning programs have consisted of recordings and vocal numbers by a quartette composed of Helen Sykora, Helen Melsha, Mildred Mahring, and Henrietta Kubik. Between the musical selections, in addition to the usual advertising, announcements have been given in the Czech language of meetings of organizations, social affairs, and lectures.[72]

Dramatic Organizations

The first Czech dramatic productions, as previously noted, were presented by the Reading Society in 1869 in Brown's Hall and in 1870 in the Society's own hall. After 1872 the Thalee Society also showed its love of the drama by the presentation of occasional plays. Soon after 1870 the dramatic club of the Reading Society, which then existed as an individual unit within that organization, appointed committees to present plays every second Monday night in the hall.

---

[71] This information was obtained from a scrapbook of undated clippings in the possession of the Czech Fine Arts Association.
[72] This information was secured from Miss Alice Spevacek and T.B. Hlubucek.

Sometimes these productions were comedies and dramas translated into the Czech language from other tongues, but more often they were their own national dramas presented in quaint costumes or operettas gay with national songs and dances. The two most outstanding plays which were presented between 1879 and 1881 were "Cesta kolem světa" (A Journey Around the World) and "Rip Van Winkle". An example of the participation of this dramatic society in civic affairs is shown by its presentation of two plays, "Jan Žižka z Trocnova" (Jan Zizka of Trocnov) and "Dvě sirotci" (Two Orphans), in 1891 at Greene's Opera House for the benefit of Saint Luke's Hospital which was then being erected in Cedar Rapids.[73]

From 1890 to 1891 this group of amateur actors was affiliated with the Lyra choral society and from that year to 1902 with the Česká Beseda club. Not daunted by the collapse of that organization, those persons from the Reading Society, the Sokols, and the Prokop Velký Lodge who were particularly interested in dramatic productions then formed their own group of amateur actors and presented plays first in one hall and then in another. These plays were always followed by dances and often the two festivities interfered with each other because those who came to dance were not usually interested in the dramatic productions. Realizing, therefore, that it would be best to present plays unaccompanied by dances, these amateur performers met at the close of the play season of 1900 and organized a new dramatic society known as the Ochotnické Družstvo (Amateur Dramatic Society).[74]

For forty-three years this organization has continued to present three or four plays in the CSPS Hall each year. All

[73] Vaclav Janda's "Ochotnické Družstvo" in *Památník česko-amerického dne při zlatém jubileu města Cedar Rapids, 14 června, 1906*, p. 29; *The Cedar Rapids Republican*, February 7, 1915.
[74] Janda's "Ochotnické Družstvo" in *Památník česko-amerického dne při zlatém jubileu města Cedar Rapids, 14 června, 1906*, p. 29.

actors, managers, and ushers have donated their services and admission fees have been just large enough to cover the expense of producing the play and purchasing new properties. As a result, the society has secured thousands of dollars worth of properties and scenery. Much of this scenery, which has been painted by local artists, produces an old world atmosphere because it pictures the houses, street scenes, and landscapes of old Bohemia.[75]

Another Czech dramatic club in Cedar Rapids which still exists is the Česká Lípa (Czech Linden) club of Saint Wenceslaus Catholic Church. It was organized on October 7, 1892, by Father Kopecky and Josef Miska with eighteen charter members. The purpose of the organization has been to promote a love for the Czech drama, to provide entertainment for the young people, and to present an opportunity whereby amateur actors may express themselves in the Czech language. Three or four plays a year of various types have been presented to appreciative audiences in the school assembly room or, on special occasions, in the CSPS Hall. The proceeds from these plays have been used for the purchase of stage equipment, a piano for the hall, and text books for the Saint Wenceslaus School.[76]

The latest dramatic society to be organized among the Czech people is the Dramatický Kroužek (Dramatic Circle) founded in 1932 as an auxiliary of the ZCBJ Lodge. It has maintained its status independently of the lodge although its members are also members of the lodge. During the first few years of its existence six plays were presented annually; at the present time three or four are staged each year at the ZCBJ Hall. M.L. Hromadka, the present president of the

---

[75] *The Cedar Rapids Republican*, September 13, 1914, October 24, 1915, February 13, 1916. Information was also secured from Milvoj Hasek and Theodore Hlubucek, both of whom have acted in many plays. The writer has seen several of the Czech plays.

[76] *Letopisy Saint Wenceslaus Golden Jubilee*, 1924, p. 36. Information was also secured from Monsignor August Vojacek.

Dramatický Kroužek, attributes this annual decrease in the number of stage productions, not to any lack of interest, but to the increasing difficulty of securing men who have time to devote to play rehearsals.

All three of the Czech dramatic societies have certain characteristics in common. All create their own scenery when it is needed; in all, old and young participate in the same production with children and adults alike taking appropriate parts; all use a European custom of having the prompter's box at the front of the stage, just below stage level, and protected from the audience by a small shell-shaped screen; all produce plays to maintain among their people the beauty of the Czech drama and to give to those of that descent an idea of the country of their ancestors.[77]

Other Cultural Organizations

Some of the other cultural organizations of the Czechs also supported dramatic productions. One of these was the Česká Beseda, founded in 1891, by a group of thirty men "to improve the knowledge of its members in Czech national culture through music and dramatizations." Women were admitted as members at the second meeting of the society. Unlike the other dramatic organizations where directors of the plays received no remuneration, in the Česká Beseda club they were paid five dollars to direct a two-act play and ten dollars for a three-act play. The music director received two dollars for the presentation of an opera. The first public program given by the society was an opera, "Král Vondráček" (King Vondracek), which was presented in May, 1891, under the direction of Josef Tlapa. It earned a profit of $65.70.[78]

[77] This information was secured from M.L. Hromadka.
[78] By-laws of the Česká Beseda Club; Minutes of the Česká Beseda Club, January 18 to June 14, 1891.

Activities of the organization were varied. In 1891 this club contributed to the Saint Luke's Hospital fund. There were picnics in Frank Mitvalsky's woods, a party for the benefit of the Czech school, dances, and plays. Gradually, however, the latter were superseded by social activities. In March, 1901, it was decided to have Sunday programs of Czech readings and music and to assemble each Friday night to learn the beseda, the national dance of the Czech people. Interest in the organization declined, however, and in June, 1902, it was disbanded. The rug and other properties of the Česká Beseda club were given to the Czech school.[79]

The Minerva Society, which still exists, is a cultural organization of a different type. It was founded in November, 1901, by fourteen young Czech women in response to a call from Jennie Hasek and Anna Kurka to discuss the organization of a literary club. A rule was adopted at one of the first meetings of the society and adhered to for years that half the program was to be in the Czech language and half in English. Topics studied by the club in its regular meetings have included: Czech literature and history, English literature, Czech music, Russian and Polish history, American history, American and European cities, and such books as *Bohemia and the Cechs* and *Masaryk's Own Story*. The society still holds occasional meetings but the programs now, with the exception of a few Czech poems and stories, are given in the English language.[80]

The newest cultural organization is the Czech Fine Arts Association. In the early 1930s about twenty Czech students who had graduated from the Czech school asked for an organization to further their study of the music and literature of Czechoslovakia. A society, sponsored by Mrs. J.J. Hervert and T.B. Hlubucek, was therefore formed, known as the Wednesday Czech Group. In 1933 this club was reorganized,

[79] Minutes of the Česká Beseda Club, June 2, 1902.
[80] A report of this organization was given to the writer by Miss Anna Kurka, the present secretary of the organization.

adults were included in its membership, and it became known as the Czech Fine Arts Society. It is an English-speaking organization which meets to discuss current topics, to enjoy Czech music, and to study various phases of the culture of Czechoslovakia. Recently the society revived the beseda dance which is popular not only among Czech people but also among other citizens.[81]

In order that they might be more united in their activities, the Czech people of the city formed the Czech Alliance in 1935. It is a federation of thirty-two cultural, fraternal, religious, and civic groups in Cedar Rapids. Other purposes of the Alliance have been to eliminate rivalry among the groups, to represent all of the Czechs before the American public, and to sponsor lectures and programs. Since its organization, its achievements have been varied. One was the sponsorship which it assumed of the Sunday Czech radio program. Another was a market held in the spring of 1939 for the sale of Czech goods. The articles for sale, all of which had been obtained from Czechoslovakia through the Czech National Alliance, included linen, glass, jewelry, and toys. A sum of $2,000 which was cleared in one week was sent to the Czech National Alliance.[82]

Another achievement of the local organization was a proclamation issued by Governor Nelson G. Kraschel which established October 28th as Czech Day in the state. The first observance of this day in Cedar Rapids was in 1937. At that time a program of music and addresses was presented in the CSPS Hall. A distinguished speaker for the occasion was Honorable Charles Cervenka, Czechoslovak consul at Chicago. Two years later Dr. Alice Masaryk was in the city for Czech Day and lectured in her native tongue to a large assembly of Czechs at the CSPS Hall.[83]

---

[81] This report was secured from T.B. Hlubucek and Mrs. J.J. Hervert.
[82] This report was secured from T.B. Hlubucek.
[83] This information was secured from Mrs. Joseph Felter.

In addition to these annual observances of October 28th, other programs have been presented under the auspices of the Czech Alliance. Two of these have been of special interest to Cedar Rapids citizens. One was a lecture in the fall of 1940 delivered by Jan Masaryk, son of the former president of Czechoslovakia, to an audience of several thousand people in the Memorial Building. The other was a concert, March 18, 1942, presented in the same place by the Coe College military band as a memorial to Thomas G. Masaryk whose birthday was March 7th. [84]

The local alliance cooperated with various national Czech organizations. In 1941 it contributed $2,000 to the American Friends of Czechoslovakia society. This is an organization to assist exiles from that country to find new homes in other lands, to inform American people of developments of Czechoslovakia, and to maintain cultural contacts between the people of the United States and Czechoslovakia.[85]

Another organization with which the local alliance has cooperated is the Czech National Alliance, founded during the First World War and reorganized at the outbreak of the Second World War. One purpose of the organization is to secure the participation of all citizens of Czech descent in the cultural, social, and political development of America. A second purpose is to disseminate, especially among the young people, an affection for the cultural heritage and language of the Czechs. A third purpose is to work for the re-establishment of the freedom and independence of Czechoslovakia.[86]

In order to collect funds for this national organization, the local alliance has sponsored annual bazaars. Financially the one in 1940 was the most successful since the bazaar of

---

[84] News item in *The Cedar Rapids Gazette*, March 15, 1942.
[85] This information was secured from T.B. Hlubucek and the by-laws of the American Friends of Czechoslovakia society.
[86] By-laws of the Czech National Alliance.

1918. As a result of it, $5,000 was earned and sent to the headquarters of the Czech National Alliance in Chicago. In addition to the bazaars, contributions for the National Alliance are secured from individual donors whose names are recorded in a book called the *Zlatá Kniha* (Golden Book).[87]

Other groups of Czech people have offered the citizens of Cedar Rapids worthwhile contributions. One, for example, which was given under the auspices of the Jan Hus Memorial Presbyterian Church and the Czech Reformed Church, was the observance of the three hundred and fiftieth anniversary of the birth of Jan Amos Komensky. In the afternoon of March 29, 1942, at a vesper service at Coe College, Dr. Matthew Spinka of Chicago lectured in English concerning the life of the famous Czech educator. In the evening he conducted services in the Czech language in the Jan Hus Memorial Presbyterian Church.[88]

The Sokols

The Sokol organization is the only Czech organization in the United States which had its origin in Bohemia.[89] The word "Sokol" means "falcon", a bird which typifies swiftness and freedom. The society was founded in 1862 by Jindrich Fuegner and Dr. Miroslav Tyrš. The latter expressed the ideals of the organization when he said:

> "Sokol does not mean physical training only –
> Sokol's aim is to educate our people to the highest
> physical efficiency, to nobleness, and to morality....
> When we address a Sokol the response will come from a
> man in the truest sense of the word – a man physically,

---

[87] This material concerning the collection of funds was secured from T.B. Hlubucek and William Valenta.

[88] News item in *The Cedar Rapids Gazette*, March 22, 1942.

[89] Rosicky's *A History of the Czechs in Nebraska*, p. 352.

50

mentally and morally – a Patriot who is ever ready to respond to the call of his country, ever ready to draw the sword in defense of Democracy, Liberty, and Humanity."[90]

Instilled with these principles, a group of Czechs in 1865 founded in St. Louis the first Sokol organization in the United States. Four years later Josef Sommer organized a gymnastic club in Cedar Rapids as an auxiliary group of the Reading Society. Mr. Sommer's death in the summer of 1870 temporarily checked the gymnastic activities of the local club, but after an interim of three years a small group of men who were interested in gymnastic training gathered in the Reading Society Hall on June 6, 1873, and founded the Jednota Tyrš, a Sokol organization.[91]

A membership of twenty-nine persons at that time soon increased to seventy. Drilling apparatus which was purchased with funds received from various collections was installed in the hall of the Reading Society and there drills were conducted on Monday, Wednesday, and Friday evenings with Karel Polansky as instructor. The local organization accepted the by-laws and constitution of the Sokols in Racine and, after 1878, wore the uniform of the majority of the Sokols in the United States. Out of respect to those "boys in blue" who fought in the Civil War, this uniform was a navy blue suit with a broad-brimmed blue hat. The uniform worn by the Sokols in Bohemia and by the members in some of the American cities consisted of a gray suit, red shirt, and a small round black cap with a falcon's feather.[92]

---

[90] Joseph Cermak's *Dr. Miroslav Tyrš*, pp. 9, 10.
[91] Will S. Monroe's *Bohemia and the Cechs*, p. 191; Hrbkova's "Bohemians Have Done Much for Cedar Rapids" in *The Cedar Rapids Republican Semi-Centennial Magazine Edition*, June 10, 1906. Jednota Tyrš literally means Tyrš organization.
[92] Boleslav Trojan's *"Paměti českých osadníku v Americe"* in *Amerikán Národní Kalendář*, 1927, p. 243; Cermak's *Dr. Miroslav Tyrš*, p. 17. After 1917 these two Sokol organizations combined to form the American Sokol Union.

The Jednota Tyrš society also sponsored picnics, dances, and a form of health insurance. The importance of the picnics may be judged from a statement in the first constitution of the organization which said that members of the society would be fined twenty-five cents each time they failed to attend a monthly meeting and one dollar if they did not go to a picnic. If a member were not present at four monthly meetings or two picnics and had no valid excuse his name would be dropped from the list of members.

Another social activity was the annual Šibřinky,[93] or masquerade dance, which was held the Monday preceding Ash Wednesday. This dance originated among the Sokols in Bohemia where Dr. Fuegner had felt that a masquerade party would not only provide merriment but would give people a chance to make new friends and where elaborate dances were therefore held in a hall in Prague decorated for the occasion with special scenery. Just when the Sokols of Cedar Rapids enjoyed their first Šibřinky is not known. In February, 1874, however, there is a brief account in a local newspaper of a masquerade party in which the band first paraded the streets of the city followed by a delegation of mounted masqueraders.[94]

That early organization also provided for the physical well being of its members by a simple plan for health insurance. According to the constitution of the society, if a member became ill, his fellow members were each assessed ten cents a week and from that fund insurance could be collected for a period not to exceed five weeks. If one failed to pay his assessment fee or if one pretended to be ill when he was not, he forfeited his membership in the organization.[95]

In addition to the Jednota Tyrš, a second Sokol organization was founded in March, 1876, and called the

---

[93] This word literally means *merriment*.

[94] *The Cedar Rapids Republican*, February 12, 1874, February 14, 1915.

[95] Frank Filip's "Jednota Tyrš, Cedar Rapids Sokols" in *Památník česko-amerického dne při zlatém jubileu města Cedar Rapids, 14 června, 1906*, p. 12.

Cedar Rapids Sokols. Gymnastic classes for this unit were conducted twice a week or oftener in Thalee Hall where Karel Polansky served as instructor. In the course of one year the membership of this society increased from eleven to fifty persons. In July, 1881, the Jednota Tyrš society became independent of the Reading Society with Frank Bednar as instructor of the new organization and in March, 1888, the Cedar Rapids Sokols affiliated with the Jednota Tyrš unit.[96]

For a few years after 1888 little progress was made by the local Sokols. Then in May, 1892, Jan J. Hrbek, Louis Brydl and Ferdinand Engelthaler, the new director, were instrumental in establishing an organization for women. This society, which was called the Tělocvična Jednota Sokolek Tyrš,[97] began with seventeen charter members. These women decided to drill Wednesday and Friday evenings. Four years after the organization of this Sokol society, a drill team composed of ten women represented the local organization in a national tournament in Chicago. This association was disbanded on April 26, 1898, reorganized in 1900, and renamed the Renata Tyršová[98] in August, 1914.[99]

An increase in the membership of the Sokol societies after 1892 necessitated a larger hall. Consequently a house on Seventh Avenue and Third Street was purchased, converted into a gymnasium, and opened with "a great celebration" on May 30, 1896. This building soon proved to be inadequate and an additional lot on the corner adjoining the first piece of

---

[96] *Cedar Rapids City Directory*, 1877-1878, p. 33; Filip's "Jednota Tyrš, Cedar Rapids Sokols" in *Památník česko-amerického dne při zlatém jubileu města Cedar Rapids, 14 června, 1906*, p. 12.

[97] This name literally means women's society founded by Tyrš.

[98] Renata Tyrs was the wife of Dr. Miroslav Tyrš and the daughter of Jindrich Fuegner, co-founders of the Sokols in Prague.

[99] This information was obtained from a report of the organization written by Mrs. Joseph Kralik.

property was purchased and a new Sokol hall was erected.[100] The main portion of this new building was a gymnasium, seventy-five feet square and twenty-three feet high. A gallery for spectators ran half way around it. The hall was provided with shower baths and the gymnasium was equipped with Indian clubs, dumb-bells, wands, and other physical culture apparatus.

The dedication of this new Sokol hall occurred on Sunday afternoon, January 13, 1901. The exercises opened with "The Sokol's Triumphal March", composed for the occasion by J. Dvorak. Dr. J. Rudis Jicinsky, chairman of the building committee, formally handed over the new gymnasium to the Sokol president, Josef Halq. Following that, there was a hoop drill by twenty-four girls and a wand drill by a class of boys. Mayor John Redmond spoke of the effort that the Czech people in Cedar Rapids had made to secure for themselves and their children every possible advantage. He also thanked them for their generosity in permitting children of other nationalities to drill in their gymnastic classes. At the time of the dedication of this building the Cedar Rapids Sokol unit had one hundred members and large classes for children and adults.[101]

In 1907, when the Chicago, Rock Island and Pacific Railway Company purchased three blocks of property including that of the Sokol organization, it was necessary for the local unit to consider the erection of a new building. This new hall, completed in January, 1909, on Third Street between Fourth and Fifth Avenues, is the present Sokol Hall. The gymnasium, which is on the first floor, is fifty-eight feet long and forty-six feet wide, has a gallery for spectators, and is equipped with apparatus which includes horses, bucks, rings,

[100] *The Cedar Rapids Republican*, January 17, 1909; Filip's "Jednota Tyrš, Cedar Rapids Sokols" in *Památník česko-amerického dne při zlatém jubileu města Cedar Rapids, 14 června, 1906*, p. 12.
[101] *The Cedar Rapids Republican*, January 15, 1901.

54

and bars. The second floor has a parlor for trophies and pictures and a large club room.

This building was dedicated on Sunday, January 17, 1909, and to accommodate an interested public an exhibition of the work of the Sokols was presented in the afternoon in the city auditorium rather than in the hall. It included drills with Indian clubs by a young women's class, work on apparatus by groups of boys, combined fancy marches and drills with wands and flags by one hundred boys and girls between the ages of five and ten, fencing with swords by men, and an exhibition on horizontal and parallel bars by a visiting Chicago squad of Sokols.[102]   An editor of a local paper commented:

> "In connection with the dedication, the society gave a series of exhibitions of its work that were a surprise to all who were privileged to see them.... The Sokols have set a standard that has hardly been excelled in this country.... Their aim is to develop the best in manhood and the best in citizenship. It is a society whose services are of the greatest interest and highest deserts."[103]

The statement of Sokol principles at this time included the following:

> "But we are always mindful of the fact that our aid and interest in the country of our forefathers must be carried on within the lawful limits of our own country's laws and restrictions. We firmly believe that only an exemplary American citizen can serve to bring honor and respect to the land of our fathers".[104]

---

[102] *The Cedar Rapids Republican*, January 17, 19, 1909.
[103] Editorial in *The Cedar Rapids Republican*, January 19, 1909.
[104] *American Sokol Union Constitution and By-Laws* (1939), pp. 4, 5.

In addition to the national union of Sokols, district organizations have also been established. Cedar Rapids was in the central district until 1939 when it became a part of the western division. The local unit, which is organized with the customary corps of officers, conforms to the regulations of the national and district organizations, organizes physical training classes, and hires a director to supervise these classes. Members of the local unit are men and women of Czech descent who are either citizens of the United States or who have declared their intention of becoming citizens. Gymnastic classes for young people and adults are, however, open to all.

In addition to drilling in these classes, gymnasts may compete in tournaments which are known as Slets. All-Sokol Slets were held in Prague as late as the summer of 1938; national Slets, or festivals, are held every five years, and there is an annual district Slet. A Slet consists of calisthenics, exercises on the apparatus, track events, high jumps and broad jumps, the shot put and discus throw for young men, exercises on the balance beam for women, and mass exercises for all of the participants.[105]

The social phases of the Sokol society were not neglected during the period from 1904 to 1917. Šibřinky dances became increasingly popular and more elaborate with prizes for the best masquerade costumes. At one held on March 5, 1916, fifteen awards were given to those most uniquely attired. Jansa's band played for this party which was attended by one thousand people. A dance known as the Majový Věneček (May wreath) which had its origin in Bohemia was enjoyed annually the first day of May. Eighty couples attended a typical dance in 1916 and danced the beseda dance in the CSPS Hall which was beautifully decorated with spring flowers.[106]

---

[105] This information was secured from Dr. Thomas Suchomel, past president of the local Sokols, from Mrs. Joseph Kralik, and from Miss Georgia Kopecky.
[106] *The Cedar Rapids Republican*, March 12, May 7, 1916.

In addition to the gymnastic classes and the social activities, the Sokol organization also sponsored instructive lectures for its members. These were planned by the educational committee and were given at the regular monthly meetings of the society or following the evening classes. Members were urged to read their national monthly publication, *Sokol Americký*, which discussed social problems, national affairs, educational topics, health, and the technical branch of the Sokol work.[107] There was also a local publication which the Sokols read, a magazine of a humorous nature called *Šibřinky* which was published annually just preceding the Šibřinky dance by a committee of Sokols.[108]

After 1917 interest in the gymnastic classes for men and boys was not as evident as it had been previous to that year. There are several reasons for this change. One reason was that the boys in the gymnastic classes were far more interested in competitive sports than in calisthenics and apparatus work. Another reason was that most of the young men who had been active leaders in the early 1900s fought in the First World War. After the war when they no longer drilled in the Sokol classes, there were no skilled gymnasts to take their places. Also, after 1924, when the number of Czech immigrants to the United States decreased, direct contact with the Sokols of Czechoslovakia gradually ceased. Previous to that date, new settlers in Cedar Rapids brought new ideas from their Sokol units in the "old country".[109]

In the 1930s two events indicate the activities of the Cedar Rapids Sokols. One was the establishment of a health camp three miles south of Center Point and about eighteen miles from Cedar Rapids. In 1931 Jan J. Hrbek gave this property to the local unit. During the summer a two weeks'

---

[107] *The Cedar Rapids Republican*, July 19, 1914.

[108] These magazines are still published but, according to Dr. Suchomel, they are not as widely read as they were previous to 1917.

[109] This information was furnished by Dr. Thomas Suchomel and Rudolph Novak.

camp for children is conducted, for both boys and girls, sponsored and managed by members of the local organization. In addition there are cottages, a dance pavilion, and picnic grounds at the camp which are available to all the members of the local Sokol society.[110]

Another event of importance in the 1930s was the founding on October 24, 1936, of the Junior Falcons, an organization for young people from the ages of twelve to eighteen, sponsored by members of the Renata Tyršová group. The object of this society which has no restrictions as to creed or nationality has been "to promote and enhance the social and educational welfare of the youth of pre-Sokol age and to foster and develop the ideals of the national Sokol organization." Since its organization, the club has held monthly business meetings followed by some activity such as skating or gymnastic exercises.[111]

In the meantime, teams of women continued to compete in national and district Slets. Between 1929 and 1942 the local organization was represented at eight Slets held in Chicago, Cleveland, Crete, Nebraska, and Cedar Rapids. In 1932 Rose Paidar was sent as a representative of the local society to the All-Sokol Slet in Prague. In 1925 the Renata Tyršová society received an autographed portrait of Renata Tyrs; in 1933 a flag and three volumes of poems came from Kolín, Czechoslovakia; in 1938 members of the local society who went to Prague to attend the All-Sokol Slet were instructed to place wreaths on the tombs of Dr. Thomas G. Masaryk and Renata Tyrs; on October 6, 1939, Dr. Alice Masaryk, who was then in Cedar Rapids, was made an honorary member of the Renata Tyršová society.[112]

With the outbreak of the war in December, 1941, the Sokol unit immediately prepared for service. Early in 1942 a

---

[110] Information furnished by Dr. Suchomel.
[111] By-laws of the Junior Falcons; minutes of the Junior Falcon organization.
[112] Reports written by Mrs. Joseph Kralik and Miss Georgia Kopecky.

58

first-aid unit and a home-nursing unit with eighty members was organized. On March 25, 1942, sixty-one Czech men registered in the Sokol Hall for a Czech Home Guard unit. One of the purposes of this organization was to drill men for military service. Rudolph Novak, a World War veteran, was named the commander. The Czech Home Guard made its first public appearance in uniform the first Sunday in June, 1942, at the Czech Memorial Day services held in the Bohemian National Cemetery. This organization which is believed to be the only Czech guard unit in the United States was accepted as part of the home defense by the local civilian defense director. Twenty-five members have left for service in the armed forces. The remainder are chiefly men over thirty-eight; others are classified as 4F. The Czech Guard serves as one of the three auxiliary police units in Cedar Rapids.[113]

Another recent event of importance was the western division Slet which was held in Cedar Rapids on June 27 and 28, 1942. Competition was between teams from Omaha and Schuyler, Nebraska, and Cedar Rapids. The mass drills at the ZCBJ Park[114] were attended by two impressive ceremonies which exemplify the Czech-American principles of the Sokols. First came the grand entry into the stadium. All the participants, headed by a group of Sokol officials, marched into position before the speaker's stand while the Czech Home Guard raised the colors and all joined in an oath of allegiance to the United States. The last event was a tribute paid to the martyrs of Lidice, Czechoslovakia. Six little girls, holding a Czech flag and bearing aloft a Lidice sign draped in mourning, took the field while the audience bowed their heads as the

---

[113] Information received from Dr. Thomas Suchomel; *The Cedar Rapids Gazette*, April 12, June 8, July 12, 1942.
[114] This park which is six miles south of Cedar Rapids belongs to the Západní Česko-Bratrská Jednota lodge.

Karla Masaryk Chorus, attired in Czech costumes, sang the Czech national anthem.[115]

Religion

The religious situation among the Czechs has been unique, for among no other immigrants who have come to the United States have so many people professed religious liberalism. The origin of this liberalism may be traced back to fifteenth-century Bohemia where the followers of Jan Hus sought to correct the abuses of the Roman Catholic Church and to offset Austrian autocracy with Czech democracy. For two centuries following Jan Hus, Protestantism was the dominant religion of Bohemia; then came the defeat of the Czechs in the Battle of White Mountain and the subsequent supremacy of Austria and the Roman Catholic Church. Many of the Protestants fled to other countries or remained in Bohemia to worship in secret, still clinging to the motto of Jan Hus, "Seek the truth, hold the truth."[116]

The Catholic religion, however, soon became the prevailing religion in Bohemia, and 96 per cent of the people professed that faith in 1920. After the Toleration Patent of 1781, issued by Joseph II of Austria, religious freedom was granted to Lutherans and Calvinists but not to the Bohemian (Moravian) Brethren. Protestants, Catholics, and free-thinkers made up the Czech immigrants to the United States.[117]

---

[115] *The Cedar Rapids Gazette*, June 27, 28, 29, 1942. The Karla Masaryk Chorus is conducted by a lodge of that name.
[116] Rosicky's *A History of the Czechs in Nebraska*, pp. 279, 285.
[117] Kenneth D. Miller's *The Czechoslovaks in America*, p. 120; Rosicky's *A History of the Czechs in Nebraska*, p. 284.

60

The Liberals or Free-thinkers

In the nineteenth century when a liberal trend reappeared in Bohemia, Charles Havlicek, with his anti-clerical ideas, led a movement against the Roman Church and some of the liberal-minded Czechs who fled from Bohemia during the Revolution of 1848 renounced a religion which to them was associated with the Austrian autocracy. They gladly welcomed the American idea of the separation of church and state.[118]

Various classes of liberals or free-thinkers appeared among the Czechs in the United States. Some were negativists; some believed in nature as the guiding force of mankind; and others had faith in a Creator but did not approve an organized church.[119] Some believed that there was no God and hence no future life. Ladimir Klacel, for example, wrote:

"There is no future,...there cannot be a heaven, and there is absolutely no hell. The heaven for which you can prepare yourself and your families is right here upon the earth."[120]

Among the early Czech settlers in Cedar Rapids there were many with liberal ideas concerning religion. Before 1868 they met in friendly gatherings to discuss their beliefs; after that year, as members of the Reading Society, they congregated in a more formal organization to investigate and debate new thoughts concerning liberalism. It was in one of those gatherings that Jaroslav Vostrovsky and Jakub Polak suggested that steps be taken to have the newspaper *Pokrok*,

[118] Francis J. Brown and J.S. Roucek's *Our Racial and National Minorities*, p. 236.
[119] Rosicky's *A History of the Czechs in Nebraska*, p. 279; Boleslav Trojan's "Paměti českých osadníku v Americe" in *Amerikán Národní Kalendář*, 1927, p. 245.
[120] *The Cedar Rapids Republican*, September 30, 1906. Ladimir Klacel, an ex-monk, was buried in Belle Plaine, Iowa.

then published at Racine, Wisconsin, transferred to Cedar Rapids.[121] Their efforts were successful and for two years, 1869 to 1871, Frank B. Zdrubek, a militant atheist, edited the paper in the Iowa community.

After the completion of the Reading Society Hall in 1870, these people gathered there on Saturday nights and on Sundays to listen to lectures given by Mr. Zdrubek. During that same year, through the efforts of this famous journalist, there was organized in Cedar Rapids the first official unit of the České Svobodné Obce (Society of Free-thinkers) in the United States. An outstanding event during Mr. Zdrubek's short residence in Cedar Rapids was his lecture in commemoration of the work of Thomas Paine.[122]

When *Pokrok* was moved to Cleveland, Ohio, the society of liberals in Cedar Rapids suffered a set-back. Few capable speakers could be secured in those days aside from the teacher, John B. Suster. The founding of the Sokols and the fraternal organizations temporarily strengthened the power of the liberals, for the members of those early societies were largely free-thinkers, although these organizations did little to aid the congregation of the liberals directly.

In the late 1870s and 1880s new settlers and visitors who came to Cedar Rapids again aroused interest in liberalism, both political and religious. One was Josef Urban, a socialist. He organized a group of one hundred laborers who, through the efforts of their ardent apostle, also became free-thinkers. As a lecturer Urban attracted attention because of his fiery comments. Sometime after 1877 L.J. Palda, "the father of Cech socialism" in the United States, moved to Cedar Rapids. During the winter of 1880, interested audiences listened each

[121] L.J. Palda's "Ruch svobodomyslný v Cedar Rapids, Ia." in *Památník česko-amerického dne při zlatém jubileu města Cedar Rapids, 14 června, 1906*, p. 10.
[122] Trojan's "Paměti českých osadníku v Americe" in *Amerikán Národní Kalendář*, 1927, pp. 243-245; L.J. Palda's "Sin čtenářského spolku v Cedar Rapids, Iowa", in *Květy Americké*, Vol. III, p. 160.

Sunday afternoon to the lectures of this eloquent speaker, but when spring came regular lectures were again abandoned.[123]

In the early 1900s an organization of liberals was again started in Cedar Rapids known as the Svobodomyslný Družstvo (Free-thinking Society of Czechs), the purpose of which was to sponsor educational lectures. Once a month there were discussions in the CSPS Hall[124] concerning Thomas Paine, Robert Ingersoll, Jan Amos Komensky, and various religious denominations. The membership of the congregation numbered about one hundred people.

The speaker was Joseph J. Hajek, one of the most capable leaders the society ever had. Mr. Hajek had studied at the University of Prague before he came to the United States to become the editor of a Czech newspaper. He wrote poetry and two volumes of speeches to be used by liberal speakers. The new free-thinkers' society was incorporated under the laws of the state and Hajek was authorized to solemnize marriages. He also conducted funeral services and named children.[125]

After the death of Mr. Hajek in 1930, lectures were no longer given. Young people were not interested in the doctrines of the free-thinkers and the liberal faith of most of the people was of a negative quality. Some became members of the Liberal Christian (Unitarian) Church. Because a number of the Czech people in Cedar Rapids prefer not to have a minister or a priest conduct a funeral service, a speaker occasionally performs that duty.[126]

---

[123] Thomas Capek's *The Cechs in America*, p. 194; L.J. Palda's "Ruch svobodomyslný v Cedar Rapids, Ia." in *Památník česko-amerického dne při zlatém jubileu města Cedar Rapids, 14 června, 1906*, p. 10.

[124] These initials represent the words Česko-Slovanská Podporující Spolku, the name of a benevolent society.

[125] Luther Brewer's *History of Linn County, Iowa*, Vol. II, pp. 713, 714.

[126] This information was furnished by Milvoj Hasek, a charter member of the congregation of free-thinkers.

Czech Catholic Churches

Saint Wenceslaus Catholic Church. – The early Czech Catholics in Cedar Rapids attended Saint Mary's Catholic Church[127] and occasionally Father Clement J.G. Lowery of that church invited Czech missionaries to speak to these people in their native tongue. In 1873 Father Francis Chmelar, who had parishes in nearby towns, offered to aid these Czechs to build their own church. A lot was purchased in January, 1874, and a few months later work was begun on the new structure the cornerstone of which was laid on Sunday, August 23, 1874.

On that day a procession marched from Saint Mary's Church to the site of the new church which was named Saint Wenceslaus Catholic Church. Father Chmelar addressed the audience in the Bohemian language. This address was followed by one by Father Lowery after which the cornerstone was laid with the usual ceremonies of the church. In the box below the stone were deposited current copies of Czech and American newspapers, names of municipal officers, a record of the officiating priests, current coins, and a list of the members of the congregation.[128] The building, completed in 1882, was a brick structure seventy-five feet long and twenty-seven feet wide and stood on the site of the present Saint Wenceslaus high school building.[129]

Father Chmelar advised the people of his congregation to purchase a cemetery because the money received from it could be used to maintain the school. The chance for this came in 1881 when Saint Mary's Church sold Saint John's Cemetery to the Czech parish. In the years 1880 and 1881 a church bell

[127] This is now called the Immaculate Conception Church.
[128] Florian Svrdlik's "Počátkové osady sv. Václava a její vzrůst" in *Památník česko-amerického dne při zlatém jubileu města Cedar Rapids, 14 června, 1906*, p. 14; *The Cedar Rapids Times*, August 27, 1874.
[129] *Letopisy Saint Wenceslaus Church.* This is a report of the church issued in pamphlet form.

64

was placed in a tower in front of the church and collections were made for the altar, a statue of Saint Joseph, and other church needs.[130]

Reverend John Broz served Saint Wenceslaus Church from 1889 to 1891. He was the only one of the priests trained for the priesthood in the United States; all the others were born and educated in Bohemia.[131] The next priest, Father Frank Kopecky, recognized the need for a new school building and proceeded to plan for one. In 1892, a small house adjoining the church was purchased and temporarily used for a school; two years later a brick structure was completed where five Sisters of Mercy served as teachers.[132]

Reverend Florian Svrdlik said his first mass in the local church on Saint Mary's Day, 1900. One of the most important events of his priesthood was the erection of a new church building. Need for it was evident because, during the mass services, parishioners stood in the street around the church. By 1903 a total of $10,000 had been collected. Lots north of the school were purchased and contracts were let for the church and its furnishings and also for a Sisters' home.[133]

The cornerstone of the new building was laid on August 5, 1904. A procession, headed by a platoon of police and Kubicek's Band, marched to the church site. Father Gunn of the Immaculate Conception Church laid the cornerstone assisted by seven other priests. After the sermons and addresses, the band adjourned to the school yard and

---

[130] Edward R. Burkhalter's "History of the Early Churches in Cedar Rapids, Iowa"; Svrdlik's "Počátkové osady sv. Václava a její vzrůst" in *Památník česko-amerického dne při zlatém jubileu města Cedar Rapids, 14 června, 1906*, p. 14.
[131] This information was secured from Monsignor Vojacek.
[132] Luther Brewer and B.L. Wick's *History of Linn County, Iowa*, Vol. I, p. 405.
[133] Svrdlik's "Počátkové osady sv. Václava a její vzrůst" in *Památník česko-amerického dne při zlatém jubileu města Cedar Rapids, 14 června, 1906*, p. 16.

continued to play Czech and American airs.[134] Work on the edifice continued rapidly and Christmas Day was observed in the new church. The building, which cost $40,000, was dedicated on October 18, 1905, by Archbishop John J. Keane.[135]

In 1909 the city purchased land next to the Sinclair Packing Plant for a park and sold the church a lot where a new parish house was erected; in 1910 a pipe organ was installed in the church. The present priest, Monsignor Vojacek, came to the city in 1920 and since then has worked diligently to develop the religious and educational activities of the parish.[136]

Organizations of three types have played an important part in the progress of the church. From 1882 to 1924 nine insurance, four recreational, and six religious organizations were founded, most of which are still in existence. Societies of a Czech nationalistic character are the Česká Lípa club, a Singers' Club, which gives public concerts of Czech music, and the Catholic Sokols. The latter, founded in 1910 by Frank and John Hac, added a girls' unit in 1912.

In all of the early services of the church the Czech language was used entirely to address the people but about 1927, because of a request from the young people of the parish, Monsignor Vojacek began to use the English language also. At the present time the Czech language is used in addressing the people at devotions during the week and for one service on Sunday, while for the other two Sunday services the English language is used.[137]

---

[134] *The Cedar Rapids Evening Times*, August 7, 1904.

[135] Svrdlik's "Počátkové osady sv. Václava a její vzrůst" in *Památník česko-amerického dne při zlatém jubileu města Cedar Rapids, 14 června, 1906*, p. 18.

[136] *Letopisy Saint Wenceslaus Church*; Mathias Hoffmann's *Centennial History of the Arch-diocese of Dubuque*, p. 238. The school maintained by St. Wenceslaus Church is described below.

[137] *Letopisy Saint Wenceslaus Church*; information from Monsignor Vojacek.

The Saint Ludmila Catholic Church. – In 1906 Reverend Florian Svrdlik, the priest of the Saint Wenceslaus Church, and John Viktor bought five acres of land on J Street near Wilson Avenue SW for $2800. The house on this land was rented and no further steps were taken toward the establishment of a school until 1914 when the Sisters De Notre Dame, all of whom were Czechs, announced that they would take charge of a school for the Czech Catholic children of the vicinity. By the middle of October, 1914, the building was ready and school opened there with sixty pupils. A room in the Saint Ludmila School was used as a chapel, and mass was said there each Sunday morning by priests from Saint Wenceslaus Church. Sometimes people stood out of doors for this service, and sometimes a tent was set up over the porch of the building.[138]

This house was not large enough for a school and a corporation was formed on December 22, 1915, for the purpose of erecting a new building. Father Svrdlik and Mr. Viktor donated to this new organization the property which they had purchased. Work on the structure began in September, 1915, and the first mass was said on February 13, 1916, in the chapel located on the first floor of the new school building.

Two years later Father Thomas Ballon, a native of Bohemia, offered his services to the parish with no remuneration except lodging. Upon the death of Father Svrdlik in 1920, the Saint Ludmila parish received property which he had willed to that church, and for the next two years this little west side parish was again a mission of the Saint Wenceslaus Church.[139]

---

[138] *Silver Jubilee, Saint Ludmila Church* (a pamphlet published May 25, 1941), p. 16; information secured from Frank John, one of the charter members of the church.

[139] *Silver Jubilee, Saint Ludmila Church*, p. 18; Hoffmann's *Centennial History of the Arch-diocese of Dubuque*, p. 543.

On October 6, 1922, Reverend Francis Hruby, who was then the assistant pastor at the Saint Wenceslaus Church, was appointed the first regular priest of the Saint Ludmila Church. After that the parish developed rapidly. In 1925 the Sisters De Notre Dame moved from Cedar Rapids to a convent in Omaha. The parish bought their home and some additional property adjoining the school and in 1926 the present church edifice was erected at a cost of about $27,000. Frolic Field, a large area for recreation back of the church, was put into shape in 1934 and 1935, largely through the efforts of the Frolic Club. An annual festival in June, known as the Kolach Festival, is held here. It consists of a bazaar and a carnival with coffee and kolaches served free with each paid admission and is enjoyed by the whole community.[140]

Czech Protestant Churches

The Jan Hus Memorial Presbyterian Church. — In the early 1860s there was a goodly number of Czech Protestants[141] in Cedar Rapids who were known as the Evangelicals of the Reformed Church. Because of their poverty, it was years before they were able to afford a building in which to hold their religious services and in the meantime they met in homes to sing hymns in long meter to the accompaniment of a violin. Occasionally these Protestants walked to Ely, nine miles from Cedar Rapids, to hear sermons by Reverend Francis Kun, the minister of the Reformed Church in that rural community. This church, organized in 1858, was the first Czech Protestant church in the United States.[142]

---

[140] *Silver Jubilee, Saint Ludmila Church*, pp. 22-24. Information was also secured from Father Francis Hruby.
[141] Most of these people had come from the same Protestant district of Bohemia.
[142] Miller's *The Czechoslovaks in America*, p. 143.

In 1868 Miss E.J. Lund, a public school teacher, reported to her pastor, Reverend James Knox of the First Presbyterian Church, that only a few of her pupils attended any form of religious services. As a result a Sunday school for these Czech children was organized in July of that year and conducted in a small house on Seventh Avenue and Fifth Street near the Adams School. It was later held in two rooms of the Second Ward School.[143] The next move was to a building which had been used by the First Presbyterians and which stood on the corner of Second Avenue and Third Street. Mr. Kun walked from Ely to Cedar Rapids and preached in this church three or four times a year.[144]

In the year 1874, the Czech Evangelical people found a good friend in T.M. Sinclair, the owner of the packing plant where many of these people were employed. He offered them the use of a room in his factory where boxes served as seats. Here services were held for about two years. In 1878 the Hope Mission Chapel (Third Presbyterian Church) was erected on the hill back of Saint Wenceslaus Church, and here at three o'clock Sunday school classes were taught in the English language, and at four o'clock church services were conducted in the Czech language. Reverend Mr. Kun often came to preach. During that same year Reverend J.E. Szalatnay, superintendent of the Reformed Churches in Bohemia, visited the Cedar Rapids congregation. Mr. Sinclair tried to persuade him to remain as the local pastor and even guaranteed him his salary, but the minister could not comply with this request.

On September 12, 1880, with the aid of Mr. Sinclair, this little group of Protestants formally organized a Czech Reformed Church. Finally, Reverend Mr. Bonekempr, a Russian, offered to preach to the Czech congregation and

---

[143] The building was located on the site of the present Washington High School building.

[144] Vilem Siller, Vaclav Prucha, and R.M. DeCastello's *Památník českých evanjelických církvi ve Spojených Státech*, pp. 44 ff.

came to the city at the expense of Mr. Sinclair, but his knowledge of the Czech language was so poor that the members of his congregation found it difficult to understand him. He preached his last sermon on July 2, 1882. In the meantime Mr. Sinclair's sudden death, on March 24, 1881, brought sorrow to the congregation whom he had so kindly assisted.[145]

After Mr. Bonekempr's brief pastorate, the church was often aided by Reverend Edward R. Burkhalter, the minister of the First Presbyterian Church. From 1883 to 1890 Mr. Kun again preached in Hope Mission Chapel once a month. On March 10, 1889, the Czech Reformed Church was incorporated with one hundred members and in May the frame structure of the First Congregational Church was purchased for $1600 (including the seats) and moved to the corner of Ninth Avenue and Seventh Street. On July 7th this building was dedicated with sermons by Reverend Mr. Kun[146] and several American ministers. On September 29th of that same year this Reformed Church became the Fourth Presbyterian Church of Cedar Rapids.[147]

---

[145] Siller, Prucha, and DeCastello's *Památník českých evanjelických církvi ve Spojených Státech*, pp. 45, 46; information from Charles Dudycha, son of Jan Dudycha who was one of the charter members of the church and also one of the first elders.

[146] The Reverend Francis Kun who was the first Czech Protestant minister in the United States was a very unusual man. He was born in Bohemia August 30, 1825, ordained a minister in 1849, and came to the United States in 1856. For a few years he was a farmer in Tama County, Iowa. Several times before he accepted a call to Ely, Iowa, in 1860, he walked there, a distance of fifty miles, to preach. He also taught Latin and Greek at Western College, Western, Iowa, from 1870 to 1872. He was invited to move to Cedar Rapids and his salary was guaranteed by Mr. Sinclair but he did not accept. After helping to found the church in Cedar Rapids, he became its spiritual adviser. – Frank Pokorney's "Frantisek Kun" in *Věrný služebník*, 1895, pp. 5-12.

[147] Siller, Prucha, and DeCastello's *Památník českých evanjelických církvi ve Spojených Státech*, pp. 46, 47.

In the summer of 1890 Vaclav Dudycha, a son of one of the first elders and a student at Union Theological Seminary, preached in this new church without remuneration. That fall Vaclav Hlavaty came to the United States and during the Christmas holidays preached to the people of the Fourth Presbyterian Church. On January 7, 1891, he received a call to be their minister and on January 25th he was ordained. A few months after Mr. Hlavaty's ordination, a debt of $735 on the church property was paid with the help of the First and Second Presbyterian Churches. After a thirty-year struggle to attain their goal, the people of this congregation at last had their own place of worship and a regular minister of their own nationality.[148]

Reverend Mr. Hlavaty's ministry was an epoch of progress for the church. The church membership increased from 90 in 1891 to 220 in 1900. In the fall of 1892 a church parsonage was erected at a cost of $1600. Until 1910 the church was a member of the Cedar Rapids Presbytery; in that year it became a part of the newly organized Central West Bohemian Presbytery. In 1915, the old church building was sold and moved away to make room for the new structure and on July 6th, Jan Hus Day, ground was broken for the new Bohemian Presbyterian Church, renamed the Jan Hus Memorial Presbyterian Church, which was erected at a cost of $24,000. It was dedicated on Sunday, January 9, 1916, free from debt. Dr. Joseph Bren preached the dedicatory sermon.[149]

---

[148] Information was secured from Reverend Vaclav Dudycha; Siller, Prucha, and DeCastello's *Památník českých evanjelických církvi ve Spojených Státech*, p. 47.

[149] Siller, Prucha, and DeCastello's *Památník českých evanjelických církvi ve Spojených Státech*, p. 47; *The Cedar Rapids Gazette*, January 1, 1901; John F. Hinkhouse and William M. Evans's *One Hundred Years of the Iowa Presbyterian Church*, p. 309; *The Cedar Rapids Republican*, July 11, 1915, January 9, 1916.

Reverend Vaclav Hlavaty was succeeded on January 1, 1920, by Dr. Joseph Bren, a native of Bohemia and a graduate of Union Theological Seminary in New York. During his ministry which lasted until 1938, the Boy's Club and the Girl's Club, both independent of the Young People's Society, were organized. The next minister was the Reverend Benjamin Paroulek who was born and educated in the United States. He did much to build up the primary department of the Sunday school and he instituted in it the latest methods of religious instruction. In October, 1941, the present pastor, Reverend Zdenek Pauk, who was born and educated in Czechoslovakia, came to the city.

In the first church the Czech language was the only one used; later the ministers preached sermons in English once a month. Since January, 1942, there have been two Sunday morning services, one in the English language and the other in Czech. The latter, however, still has the larger attendance. The membership of the church in June, 1942, was 190 of whom about 90 per cent were of Czech descent.[150]

The John Hus Methodist Church. – Like the Jan Hus Memorial Presbyterian Church, the John Hus Methodist Church also had a humble beginning. In the year 1890 the young people of Saint Paul's Methodist Episcopal Church in Cedar Rapids founded a mission for Czech Protestants. This was conducted in a vacant store building located on the corner of Tenth Avenue and Second Street SE. A young man by the name of Jan Tauchen, who had been a bank clerk in Chicago, volunteered to work as a missionary among the Czechs and for this purpose a chapel, known as Epworth Mission, was built on Eighth Avenue and Ninth Street. The congregation, numbering twelve members, dedicated this building on May 22, 1892. It was said to be "the first Bohemian Methodist

[150] This information was secured from Dr. Joseph Bren and Reverend Zdenek Pauk.

72

Church ever organized in this or any other country."[151] Young people met on Wednesday nights to sing, and a prayer meeting was held every Thursday night. A Sunday school was founded in May, 1892, which soon had seventy pupils; and a Young People's Society was organized which in a short time increased from six to thirty members.

On March 8, 1894, the chapel was moved to the corner of Eleventh Avenue and Seventh Street, rebuilt, and dedicated as Hus Chapel. A newspaper item commented that "the dedicatory program was well rendered and that 'Jesus, Lover of My Soul' was sung heartily in Bohemian." Reverend V. Vanek of Chicago, who gave the main address, spoke of the zeal of the Czech Protestants and of the devotion of Jan Hus. He asked for a liberal subscription to defray the expenses of moving the chapel and almost $150 was received.[152] Reverend Jan Tauchen died on March 7, 1895, and for the next three months the church was without a minister. During that interval, however, religious services were conducted by Josef Karban, one of the active members of the church.

Reverend R.N. DeCastello came to the church in July of that year. He was immediately confronted with the problem of the location of the church building, for by that time most of the members of the congregation lived on the west side of the river. Two lots on First Street and Fourteenth Avenue SW were purchased for $500. Then a vacated church building was secured from the Second Evangelical congregation and moved to one of the new lots. The price of the building was $300 which included the bell, organ, seats, and a carpet; the cost of moving and repairing it was $1500. The remodeled church was dedicated on November 14, 1897, with a Czech service in the morning, an English service in the afternoon, and another Czech service in the evening. A small library was opened in the basement of the church with 150 books in English and

---

[151] Siller, Prucha, and DeCastello's *Památník českých evanjelických církvi ve Spojených Státech*, pp. 269, 270; *The Cedar Rapids Times*, June 2, 1892.
[152] *The Cedar Rapids Times*, March 9, 1894.

Czech, but later it was closed because of disturbances in the neighborhood.[153]

In July, 1899, Reverend Frank Zavodsky became the minister and in November, 1914, he was succeeded by Reverend F.D. Chada. The latter was the last Czech pastor of the John Hus Methodist Church. During his ministry he preached in the Czech language at Sunday morning services and in English at the evening services. The membership of the church in July, 1942, was about 125 persons, 30 per cent of whom were of Czech descent.[154]

The Czech Reformed Church. – The founding of the Czech Reformed Church in Cedar Rapids was due to the fact that many members of the Ely church had moved to Cedar Rapids and wished to organize a branch of their mother congregation. Reverend Joseph Balcar, then pastor of the Independent Reformed Church at Ely, was asked by Reverend F.S. Bromer, pastor of the First Reformed Church in Cedar Rapids, to preach to the Czech people, and for that purpose he offered him the use of his church edifice.

Reverend Mr. Balcar gladly assented and the following Sunday afternoon, April 7, 1907, the first services were held and on October 3, 1909, the church was formally organized with forty-two members. The newly organized congregation continued to assemble in the building of the First Reformed Church until June 19, 1910, when for the first time it met in a tent called "Bohemian tabernacle" which had been temporarily erected until a permanent building could be provided.[155]

---

[153] Siller, Prucha, and DeCastello's *Památník českých evanjelických církvi ve Spojených Státech*, pp. 271-274.

[154] This information was secured from Reverend F.O. Hillman.

[155] The material for an account of this church was secured from an unpublished report written in Czech by Reverend Matthew Spinka in *Memorial Book of the Czech Evangelical and Reformed Church* and translated by Reverend Milo Filipi.

Early in the month of September, 1910, steps were taken for the erection of a church. Rudolph Kriz donated a lot, Charles B. Zalesky drew up the plans, and Wesley Chihak received the contract to build a church for the sum of $3800. A loan of $2700 was received from the Board of Home Missions of the Reformed Church and the remainder of the cost of the building was paid before the church was dedicated. The cornerstone was laid on Sunday, November 6, 1910, and in less than a month services were held in the basement of the building. On January 15, 1911, the church was dedicated, with all debts paid.

About two years later Reverend Joseph Balcar resigned and for a few months the church was without a pastor. Then in the spring of 1914 Matthew Spinka, a student at the Chicago Theological Seminary, was asked to supply the pulpit during the summer. After his graduation from the seminary he was ordained and installed, June 27, 1915, as the pastor of the church. Three years later he resigned and was succeeded in September, 1919, by Reverend Jaroslav T. Stulo who remained until May, 1922. During his pastorate a manse was erected. After Reverend Frank Helmich had served as minister for seventeen years, Reverend Milo Filipi was elected pastor in the fall of 1939.

In July, 1942, the church had sixty-three members, all of whom were of Czech descent. Since the Reformed Church united with the Evangelical Synod of North America in 1935, the church is now known as the Czech Evangelical and Reformed Church. Because the membership is not very large, the pastor's salary is supplemented by a yearly grant from the Board of National Missions of the Evangelical and Reformed Church. Sunday morning services are conducted in the Czech language, the Sunday school and Young People's Society are in English, and occasionally evening services are also conducted in that language.[156]

---

[156] This information was secured from Reverend Milo Filipi.

Fraternal Organizations

Soon after the early Czech settlers in the United States had erected their homes, they sought protection for themselves and their families through benevolent organizations. The first of these lodges was founded in 1850 with headquarters in New York City. About two years after it disbanded there was organized, in 1854, in St. Louis the first permanent Czech benevolent society known as the Česko-Slovanská Podporující Spolku. [*Editor's note:* The name of this organization varies from one publication to another, but all of them refer to the same entity which is generally referred to by its initials ČSPS. Some variants include *Česko-Slovanská Podporující Společnost, Česko-Slovanské Podporující Společnost,* and *Česko-Slovenský Podporující Spolek.* The variants used in this edition are the same as those in the original two volumes of *The History of Czechs in Cedar Rapids.* Even these two volumes differed slightly with each other.] Since then numerous fraternal organizations have been founded by the Czech people.[157]

The Česko-Slovanská Podporující Spolku

Fourteen years after the Česko-Slovanská Podporující Spolku (Czech Slavonian Benevolent Association) was founded in St. Louis, a group of Czech men in Cedar Rapids recognized a need for a similar organization and a meeting was summoned for June 27, 1879, in order to arrange for an alliance with the CSPS. Those present at the meeting decided to name the new organization the Prokop Velký Lodge in honor of Procopius the Great, who brought Bohemia to the

---

[157] Thomas Capek's "Czechoslovaks in the United States" in *World's Fair Memorial of the Czechoslovak Group,* p. 32.

peak of her military glory when he defeated the army of Frederick, Margrave of Brandenburg, on August 14, 1431. The request for affiliation with the CSPS was quickly acted upon by the main lodge and the local chapter received number forty-six, the first of the CSPS lodges in Iowa.[158]

The formal installation into the CSPS took place on July 27, 1879, in a building on the corner of First Avenue and First Street. At that time the annual dues of the order were six dollars. After Josef Vondracek had been received as the first candidate, the membership of this fraternal organization grew rapidly. Because there were then no Czech doctors in the city, the lodge chose Dr. Charles H. French as their official physician.[159]

Three years after the formation of the Prokop Velký Lodge, two other CSPS organizations were founded in Cedar Rapids. One, known as Karel IV Number 77, was organized on February 20, 1882, with thirty-three men and their wives as charter members. As in the Prokop Velký Lodge, this organization also adopted the name of a person famous in the history of Bohemia, Charles (Karel) IV, who was one of the best kings and truest patriots of Bohemia.[160] The second lodge organized that year, the Mladočech (Czech Youth) Number 82, was affiliated with the CSPS on December 24th with thirty-three young men as members.

From the time of its organization the Prokop Velký Lodge had planned to erect its own hall and for that purpose it

---

[158] Joseph Urban's "Jednota Česko-Slov. Podporujících Spolku" in *Památník česko-amerického dne při zlatém jubileu města Cedar Rapids, 14 června, 1906*, p. 21; Franz von Lutzow's *Bohemia*, pp. 157-160; Sarka B. Hrbkova's "Bohemians Have Done Much for Cedar Rapids" in *The Cedar Rapids Republican Semi-Centennial Magazine Edition*, June 10, 1906.

[159] Urban's "Jednota Česko-Slov. Podporujících Spolku" in *Památník česko-amerického dne při zlatém jubileu města Cedar Rapids, 14 června, 1906*, p. 21.

[160] Urban's "Jednota Česko-Slov. Podporujících Spolku" in *Památník česko-amerického dne při zlatém jubileu města Cedar Rapids, 14 června, 1906*, pp. 19, 22; Lutzow's *Bohemia*, pp. 69-73.

laid aside a definite sum of money each year. In 1881 a lot was purchased on which stands the present hall. Previous to the transaction an invitation was extended to the Karel IV and Mladočech lodges to join with Prokop Velký in the erection of the new building but both refused to do so. The Prokop Velký organization, not discouraged by this refusal, called a special meeting of its members and decided to undertake the project single handed. Contributions were made by individual members and by other Czech people in the city, a building committee was appointed, and within a short time a contract for the construction of the hall was let.

According to a newspaper account, the cornerstone was laid on October 30, 1890, "with due pomp and ceremony." In describing the event the reporter related: "The assembly was large and the procession was an imposing one." In the lead was a platoon of police, followed by a band and carriages containing Governor Horace Boies, prominent Bohemians, and the Governor's staff.

> "These were followed by a long line of the members of various Bohemian societies in regalia and carriages containing members of the female societies of the city.... The governor's address was most appropriate for the occasion, referring especially to the progress of our adopted citizens notably among whom are the Bohemians who comprise so large a number of the population of Cedar Rapids."[161]

Seven months later, on June 6, 1891, the building was dedicated. The new CSPS Hall was three stories high, cost $22,400, and was designated for the use of the lodge and other Czech societies. A large assembly room was provided, with a stage, scenery, and theatrical appliances. In order to pay a

---

[161] *The Cedar Rapids Times*, November 6, 1890.

$9000 debt on the building, bonds were issued bearing six per cent interest.[162]

Fifteen days after its dedication, June 21 to 28, 1891, the new hall was the scene of the tenth convention of the main lodge of the CSPS. There, 150 delegates from other vicinities assembled with the local members in the largest convention of Czech people which had been held in the city up to that time.[163]

In 1900 an $8000 addition, ninety feet by thirty feet, was made to the hall. The enlarged building was formally dedicated on Christmas Eve, 1900, with a dancing party attended by members of the society, their families, and a few friends. "A splendid address was given by Professor Bohumil Shimek," notes a newspaper reporter, "and at midnight an elegant supper was served." In the new addition were a reception room, a reading room, and a small lodge room. Eight years later another three-story addition to the building was completed and opened to the public, thus making the hall at that time one of the most commodious in the city.[164]

From 1915 to 1919 the CSPS Supreme Lodge was located in Cedar Rapids. During those years Dr. J.S. Vojan, the editor of the lodge magazine, *Organ C.S.P.S.*, lived in the city although the magazine was printed in Chicago.[165]

The earliest subordinate lodges of the CSPS had been founded by men although their wives were included as members. On May 14, 1927, a group of twenty-eight Czech women also demonstrated their ability as organizers when

---

[162] Urban's "Jednota Česko-Slov. Podporujících Spolku" in *Památník česko-amerického dne při zlatém jubileu města Cedar Rapids, 14 června, 1906*, pp. 21, 22.

[163] Urban's "Jednota Česko-Slov. Podporujících Spolku" in *Památník česko-amerického dne při zlatém jubileu města Cedar Rapids, 14 června, 1906*, p. 19.

[164] *The Cedar Rapids Republican*, December 27, 1900, June 28, 1909.

[165] The by-laws of the organization limit the Supreme Lodge to one city for four years at a time. See also *The Cedar Rapids Republican*, September 13, 1914, December 29, 1918.

they established their own Karla Masaryk Lodge Number 344 CSPS. The name chosen was in recognition of the services performed for Czechoslovakia by the American-born wife of Thomas G. Masaryk. The president and Mrs. Masaryk acknowledged the honor with a letter and a picture of themselves which now hangs in one of the lodge rooms of the CSPS Hall.

This organization has always supported all of the fraternal and national projects in which the Czechs of Cedar Rapids have engaged. Its outstanding achievement, however, has been the formation of the Karla Masaryk Chorus composed of ten of its members. This chorus has practiced Czech songs each Monday evening under the direction of Mrs. Esther Hronik Klersey and when it has appeared in public the members have worn authentic and colorful Czech costumes. The Karla Masaryk Chorus has sung in many concerts both in Cedar Rapids and in other Iowa communities.[166]

In 1933 the CSPS merged with four other brotherhoods to form an organization known as the Czechoslovak Society of America (CSA). Although the members of the original lodge represented the religious liberals of the Czech people, today the members are of all creeds. In Cedar Rapids in June, 1942, there were about 1500 people in the subordinate organizations of the CSA and about 1000 families received the national publication. In addition to its insurance features, the local lodges have also sponsored plays, lectures, social affairs, and bazaars.[167]

---

[166] This report was secured from Mrs. Esther Klersey.
[167] Capek's "Czechoslovaks in the United States" in *World's Fair Memorial of the Czechoslovak Group*, p. 32; information secured from T.B. Hlubucek.

Women's Fraternal Organizations

In addition to being represented in the CSPS, the ZCBJ, and the Praha Rebekah lodges, the Czech women of Cedar Rapids have been affiliated with two other national and one local fraternal organizations. These lodges are the Jednota Českých Dam (JCD), the Sesterská Podporující Jednota (SPJ), and the České Vlastenky.

The Jednota Českých Dam (Society of Czech Women) was founded in Cleveland, Ohio, on August 25, 1870, as a cultural and insurance organization. Soon subordinate branches were founded in all cities where Czech women resided. When first organized the annual dues of the lodge were two dollars. After one was a member for six months she could collect, in case of illness, two dollars per week for the first six months and one dollar per week for the second six months. In case of her death her beneficiaries received $400.[168]

The Anna Náprstek Lodge Number 24 was the first organization in Cedar Rapids to be affiliated with the national JCD. On March 9, 1884, thirty-five women assembled in the Reading Society Hall for the purpose of drawing up a constitution and by-laws, electing officers, and choosing a name for the local organization. The name of Anna Náprstek was selected in honor of a prominent Czech woman, the mother of Vojta Náprstek.

In its early days the local lodge gave two entertainments a year in order to raise money for its many and varied activities. Members of the Anna Náprstek group here called on and aided people who were ill, met and helped Czech immigrant mothers, decorated the graves of deceased members on Memorial Day, taught hand work to the girls in the Czech school, and sent contributions to Bohemia whenever

---

[168] Anna Mchovsky's *Jednota Českých Dam ve Spojených Státech Severní Ameriky*, p. 8.

droughts or floods necessitated aid. This organization still meets in the CSPS Hall once a month with an average attendance of about thirty members. Besides providing a means whereby the members may secure life insurance policies, the Anna Náprstek Lodge now provides social activities for its members, teaches patriotism, and participates in civic enterprises.[169]

The second local organization to become affiliated with the JCD was the Žofie Podlipská Lodge Number 25 which was founded in Cedar Rapids in 1885 with thirty-eight charter members. In choosing this name for their organization, says an early report of the lodge, the members wished to show that, though they were far from their homeland, they had not forgotten it and therefore they desired to honor an author of whom Bohemia was proud. By correspondence Žofie Podlipská gladly gave the Cedar Rapids lodge permission to use her name. Like the preceding organization, this lodge has also cared for the sick and needy, contributed to the Czech school, and sent donations to Bohemia.[170]

The Pomněnka Vlasti (Forget Not My Country) was the third of the JCD lodges to be organized in Cedar Rapids. Founded in 1898 with twelve members, it had one hundred members in May, 1942. It engages in practically the same activities as the other lodges affiliated with the JCD organization. One more lodge, Českých Vlastenek Number 1, joined the JCD. On May 16, 1900, it had fifty charter members.[171]

---

[169] Mchovsky's *Jednota Českých Dam ve Spojených Státech Severní Ameriky*, pp. 229-232. Information was also secured from Mrs. Marie Hurka, a charter member, and from Mrs. Anna Bohac, the present president of the lodge.

[170] Mchovsky's *Jednota Českých Dam ve Spojených Státech Severní Ameriky*, pp. 234-236.

[171] Information from Mrs. B. Hasek; "Dámské spolky v Cedar Rapids" in *Památník česko-amerického dne při zlatém jubileu města Cedar Rapids, 14 června, 1906*, p. 38.

A second national combination of lodges for Czech women is the Sesterská Podporující Jednota (SPJ) or Sisterly Benevolent Order of Lodges. The first of these to be founded in Cedar Rapids was the Hvězda Pokroku (Star of Progress) Number 4, organized on September 15, 1892. On April 19, 1897, Zdenka Havlicek Lodge Number 23 was founded, the second lodge in Cedar Rapids to be affiliated with the SPJ group. This organization was named in honor of the wife of the great Czech journalist, Charles Havlicek.[172]

In addition to organizing subordinate branches of these two national organizations, some of the Czech women of Cedar Rapids also founded a local lodge known as České Vlastenky (Czech National) Lodge. When established it had seventy members; in June, 1942, it had four hundred members. Its dues have always been ten cents a month and upon the death of a member a benefit of fifty dollars has immediately been paid to the beneficiary. Like all the other lodges, it has sponsored social activities and charitable enterprises.[173]

Jan Hus Odd Fellow and Praha Rebekah Lodges

In 1884 six Czech members of a German branch of the Odd Fellows Lodge in Cedar Rapids withdrew from that organization for the purpose of founding a Czech-speaking lodge. Five other men later joined the group and together they petitioned the Sovereign Lodge for the right to found an organization in which a Czech language ritual might be used. The request was granted and the organization was founded as

---

[172] "Dámské spolky v Cedar Rapids" in *Památník česko-amerického dne při zlatém jubileu města Cedar Rapids, 14 června, 1906*, p. 38. Information was also secured from Mrs. Joseph Paidar, an active member of both of these organizations.

[173] This information was secured from Mrs. Anton Tlusty, a charter member of the organization.

the first Czech-speaking Odd Fellows Lodge west of the Mississippi River. On March 4, 1885, it was installed, with the name of Jan Hus Number 51 IOOF, by eleven members of Lodge Palacky in Chicago. Since 1921, because of a regulation of the Sovereign Lodge, an English ritual has been used.[174]

Praha Rebekah Lodge was organized on June 23, 1888. This name was selected because many of the charter members had come from the city of Prague, Bohemia. The local lodge was a Czech-speaking organization until 1921 when all foreign language rituals were cancelled by the Sovereign Lodge. In addition to its regular lodge work, the organization's activities have included observances of Czech Victory Day (October 28th) and Mother's Day, Christmas parties, special meetings honoring past officers, and the support of its Children's Home and the Odd Fellow's Home. In 1938 one hundred candidates were initiated into the organization. A membership in June, 1942, of 632 made the local lodge the largest Rebekah lodge in the world.[175]

The Západní Česko-Bratrská Jednota

The Západní Česko-Bratrská Jednota (Western Bohemian Fraternal Association) was organized at a special convention held February 9 to 11, 1897, at Omaha, Nebraska, when a group of western lodges broke away from the CSPS. The new ZCBJ was then incorporated under the laws of Iowa on July 4, 1897, with the supreme office in Cedar Rapids. By September 30th of that year, forty-nine orders in various cities

---

[174] Vaclav Dvorak's "Jan Hus C. 51 IOOF" in *Památník česko-amerického dne při zlatém jubileu města Cedar Rapids, 14 června, 1906*, p. 40. Information was also secured from Joseph Mekota, an early member of the lodge.

[175] This information was secured from Mrs. Marie C. Novak, a prominent member of the local lodge and a state officer.

84

had joined the new alliance. This was the first Czech fraternal society to organize a lodge for young people, to institute a juvenile department, and to establish twenty-pay-life and endowment policies. The ZCBJ used the CSPS Hall for its meetings until 1908 when it erected its own hall on the corner of Third Street and Twelfth Avenue SE. The new building cost $10,000, was a three-story structure seventy feet long and fifty feet wide, and was equipped with a dance hall on the second floor and offices for the Supreme Lodge on the first floor.[176]

In 1928 the ZCBJ instituted a local festival known as a "pout". This was a revival of an "Old World" custom when on certain saints' days, Czech people went on pilgrimages to cities where cathedrals were located to attend religious services, to enjoy a puppet show, and to eat heart-shaped cookies. The ZCBJ "pout" has been held annually in May since 1928 either at the hall or at the park. There have been games for children, dances for adults, and ginger-bread cookies shaped as horses and hearts.[177]

A $22,000 addition was made to the hall in 1932 thus enlarging the stage and the portion of the building used by the Supreme Lodge. Seven years later the ZCBJ Park south of the city was purchased. Here are cottages owned by individual members of the lodge, a dance pavilion, and picnic grounds accessible to all members of the organization from May until September. The lodge owns a library of fifty books most of which deal with the benefits of insurance. It has its own magazine, *Bratrský Věstník*, which all members of the organization receive with their dues. A few pages of this publication are printed in the English language; the remainder is in Czech.[178]

---

[176] Information secured from the 1941 annual report of the lodge; *The Cedar Rapids Republican*, September 14, 15, 1908.

[177] Information secured from M.L. Hromadka, secretary of the Supreme Lodge.

[178] Information secured from M.L. Hromadka.

In Cedar Rapids five ZCBJ subordinate lodges have been organized for people of Czech descent and their families: Prokop Velký Number 7, Karel IV Number 13, Mladočech Number 15, Žižkův Dub Number 91, and Cedar Rapids Number 262. The first four were founded in 1897 and have always been Czech-speaking organizations. Three adopted the same names as lodges in the CSPS group. The name of the fourth lodge, which means Žižka's Oak, commemorates a famous leader of the Czechs during the Hussite Wars, who, according to legend, stood beneath the tree under which he had been born and "swore eternal vengeance" upon the murderers of Jan Hus.[179] The fifth in the list was founded on July 24, 1923, and is an English-speaking organization. The membership of the five lodges in June, 1942, totaled 2617 persons.

The social activities of these organizations have included dances, card parties, lectures, dramatic productions, ball games, picnics, and dinners. The ZCBJ Hall has been used by drill teams of various lodges. Since 1938 it has also been available for citizenship classes and since the spring of 1942 it has been used by a large group of Czech women engaged in Red Cross work.[180]

All these Czech benevolent organizations which are affiliated with a national lodge have, in recent years, changed the policy by which they have insured their members. The early lodges granted a uniform death or sick benefit to each member who paid dues regulated by the supreme lodges. Within the last ten years, however, these organizations have adopted a plan whereby their members have received benefits dependent upon the face value of the policies which they carry.[181]

---

[179] Lutzow's *Bohemia*, p. 117.

[180] This information was secured from M.L. Hromadka and from reports made to the writer by the five presidents of the local lodges.

[181] This information was received from T.B. Hlubucek and M.L. Hromadka.

Schools, Libraries, and the Press

"Language to the Bohemian...is history, religion, and life."[182] Because their ancestors struggled for centuries to maintain a national language and literature, these people have sought to preserve that language in the country of their adoption and they have organized schools and classes where the culture of their homeland has been taught in their native tongue to the succeeding generations. At the same time, the Czech people have welcomed opportunities to learn the language of the country they have chosen for their home.[183]

Czech-speaking Schools and Classes

Records are not available which indicate when Czech-language classes or schools were first established in Cedar Rapids. The first organization to undertake the task was the Reading Society,[184] but the minutes do not state when John B. Suster was appointed as the first teacher. Mention of his name appears in conjunction with the observance of Jan Hus Day, July 6, 1870, and in the city *Directory* for that same year.

It is probable, however, that Mr. Suster conducted a Czech school either in the Reading Society Hall or in Thalee Hall. Later, instructors taught Czech children on Saturdays, Sundays, and during the summer in Monroe and Madison public schools. Prior to 1890, a group of mothers formed an organization which, with the Reading Society, maintained these classes for the instruction of their children in the language and culture of Bohemia.[185]

---

[182] Will S. Monroe's *Bohemia and the Cechs*, p. 227.
[183] Zdenka and Jan Munzer's *We Were and We Shall Be*, pp. 14, 15.
[184] See above pages 135-140.
[185] Information secured from Milvoj Hasek and Mrs. Anton Tlusty; Ann Drahos's "Dámská Matice Školská" in *Památník česko-amerického dne při zlatém jubileu města Cedar Rapids, 14 června, 1906*, p. 31.

In the meantime another school to conduct classes in the Czech language had been established in Cedar Rapids. This was the Saint Wenceslaus parochial school which was started in 1892 in the basement of the parish house built in that year for Father Francis Chmelar. Two years later, Father Kopecky helped the parish erect the first Saint Wenceslaus school building and there the Sisters of Mercy used the English language for their academic classes and taught their children to speak, read, and write the Czech language. Sometimes the priests assisted with this instruction.[186]

In 1926 a $45,000 high school building was erected which included an assembly hall and a gymnasium. That same year this school became the first accredited Czech parish high school in the United States. All of the Saint Wenceslaus school children now learn Czech songs and prayers and each pupil in grades five through eight receives instruction twice a week in Czech grammar and composition.[187]

During the same year that the Saint Wenceslaus school began to instruct the pupils of the parish in the Czech language, there was organized in Cedar Rapids a society to plan for the erection of a Czech school building. This organization, known as the Dámská Matice Školská,[188] was founded September 26, 1892, and incorporated on March 16, 1894. By means of bazaars and programs the women built up a fund for the proposed building.

The society meanwhile supported Sunday classes for instruction in the Czech language and organized (in 1897) a library of children's books in that language. In the summer of 1900, W.F. Severa guaranteed the furniture for all of the schoolrooms and for the library. Then the Dámská Matice Školská appointed a building committee and an active drive

---

[186] *The Cedar Rapids Gazette*, January 1, 1901.

[187] Hoffmann's *Centennial History of the Arch-diocese of Dubuque*, p. 238; information from Monsignor Vojacek.

[188] The name of this organization literally means a woman's school-board for a school.

for more money added several hundred dollars to the fund already on hand.[189]

The new Matice Školská (Czech School) was dedicated on January 1, 1901, as the first building in the United States to be used exclusively for a Czech school.[190] In the evening there was a fine dedicatory program. The Matice Školská, which is still used as a Czech school, has two rooms on the first floor, each large enough to accommodate fifty-four pupils, and one in the basement for younger children. On the second floor is the library which is now maintained by the Reading Society.

After the dedication of the building, the ladies of the Dámská Matice Školská continued to have bazaars in order to pay the debt on the structure. They also planned programs in memory of famous Czech leaders such as Pavlicek, Hus, Komensky, Klacel, Zofie Podlipska, and American patriots such as Washington and Lincoln. The school was non-sectarian and free. It was divided into three grades in each of which the pupils sang Czech songs, studied the history and geography of Bohemia, and learned how to write, read, and speak the Czech language. In the early school girls were also taught, outside of the regular school hours, how to make lace, to knit, and to embroider. Regular classes were conducted on Saturday and Sunday mornings and for five weeks during the summer. The building was also used by older girls for night school classes in the Czech language.[191]

Since 1905 the Dámská Matice Školská has undertaken the maintenance of the school and has provided light, heat,

---

[189] Anna Drahos's "Dámská Matice Školská v Cedar Rapids" in *Památník česko-amerického dne při zlatém jubileu města Cedar Rapids, 14 června, 1906*, p. 32.

[190] Brewer and Wick's *History of Linn County, Iowa*, Vol. I, p. 124.

[191] Drahos's "Dámská Matice Školská v Cedar Rapids" in *Památník česko-amerického dne při zlatém jubileu města Cedar Rapids, 14 června, 1906*, p. 32; information from Mrs. Marie Chmelicek, one of the present teachers, and from Mrs. Joseph Egermeyer, one of the early teachers of the school.

repairs, and janitorial services. Funds with which to maintain the school and pay the teachers have been secured from the Czech lodges of the city and from the Sokols. A small tuition fee of fifty cents is also charged each pupil for the summer term.

Since 1905 the teachers have been appointed and the textbooks selected by the Ústřední Matice (School Board for the School), composed of two delegates chosen annually from each organization which contributes funds for the support of the school. No definite attendance records for the Matice Školská are available. A few which do exist, however, indicate a decrease in attendance since 1905.[192]

In 1912 Dr. John A. Marquis, president of Coe College, asked Dr. Anna Heyberger to teach an elective course in Czech language, culture, and literature. Down to 1918 most of the students who enrolled in these classes had a partial knowledge of the Czech language before they matriculated; they had come from homes where a grandmother, a highly respected member of the family, had instructed her grandchildren in the folklore and language of her homeland. After 1918 few college freshmen had received this type of training at home and Czech was taught only as a foreign language with emphasis on grammar rather than on the literature of Bohemia. A few years later French and German were considered the more important foreign languages, and Czech was dropped from the college curriculum.[193]

In the meantime another school opened in Cedar Rapids where instruction was received in the Czech language. In 1914 Father Florian Svrdlik offered the Sisters De Notre Dame, who had recently arrived from Horažďovice, Bohemia, a tract of land on which stood an old frame house if they would open a school for Czech children.[194] In that school the

---

[192] This information was secured from Mrs. Marie Chmelicek.
[193] This information was secured from Dr. Anna Heyberger.
[194] Hoffmann's *Centennial History of the Arch-diocese of Dubuque*, pp. 541, 640.

Sisters often addressed the children in Czech and songs were sung and prayers recited in that language. Lessons in the regular classes, however, were in English. Each Friday afternoon the girls were taught to knit and crochet and to do on samplers the colorful embroidery of Bohemia, while the boys received instruction in wood carving. Two or three times a year a program was presented consisting of a Czech play and the folksongs of Bohemia. Czech songs are still sung in all of the eight grades of the Saint Ludmila school. All of the pupils of the school are required to study the Czech language unless their parents excuse them from doing so. A choir of girls sings Czech hymns on Sunday mornings, and each Thursday morning when all of the pupils of the school attend mass, the old Catholic hymns of Bohemia are sung by the children.[195]

Between 1933 and 1935, a night school in the Czech language was conducted in the Washington High School. The Cedar Rapids Board of Education permitted the free use of the building and funds with which to pay the teachers were collected from the Czech lodges and other organizations. The students were adults and included some of the prominent Czech professional men of the city. They met to study Czech grammar, literature, history, and music. The teachers were J.C. Stepan, T.B. Hlubucek, and Frank Raska. An enrollment of eighty-five on the first night increased to two hundred students, but the classes were discontinued when plans were made for teaching the Czech language in the public schools.[196]

For several years prior to 1934 some of the prominent Czech citizens of Cedar Rapids had been urging that the language of their ancestors be taught in the public schools. The Board of Education finally consented, after a petition bearing five hundred signatures had been presented to it, and in the fall of 1934 Czech classes were organized at the Washington and Grant high schools. At the first school,

[195] Information was secured from Mrs. Zofie Kuncl Hanson, one of the first pupils of this school, and from Father Francis Hruby.
[196] This information was secured from J.C. Stepan and T.B. Hlubucek.

twenty students entered these classes the first semester and eleven the second semester while at the latter school thirty-four enrolled the first semester and eleven the second semester. The next year Washington High School had no beginning class and only thirteen students in the advanced class. At the end of the first semester therefore, the courses were dropped from the curriculum.

At the Grant School in 1935-1936 four classes of Czech were taught with an average of sixteen pupils in each class. The following year when the Grant School was divided, Czech was taught only at the Wilson School. The first semester there were eight new students, five of whom dropped the course at the end of the semester. As a result of this lack of interest during this three-year period, Czech language classes were dropped by the public schools.[197]

The Council of Higher Education

During the years when attempts were being made to introduce Czech language classes into various educational institutions in Cedar Rapids, there was founded in that city an organization to aid students of Czech descent to secure advanced education. The idea probably originated in a meeting of the Reading Society on May 29, 1901, when W.F. Severa made a motion that financial aid for an advanced education be given annually to the most capable Czech graduate of the local high school.[198]

A letter sent to the lodges concerning the matter met with no response, but on July 27, 1902, at a meeting of some of the prominent Czech citizens a temporary executive

---

[197] This information was secured from Arthur C. Deamer, superintendent of the Cedar Rapids public schools.
[198] Hrbkova's "Bohemians Have Done Much for Cedar Rapids" in *The Cedar Rapids Republican Semi-Centennial Magazine Edition*, June 10, 1906.

92

committee was elected for a new organization known as the Matice Vyššího Vzdělání (Council of Higher Education). Mr. Severa donated $2500 to the committee, "for the benefit of talented youth yearning for a higher culture."[199]

Professor Bohumil Shimek outlined the program of the organization, prepared its constitution and by-laws, and aroused interest in it by writing and lecturing about it. As a result the local fraternal organizations supported the movement with generous sums of money. The council's headquarters were at first in Cedar Rapids but they were later transferred to Chicago.[200]

According to the by-laws the objects of the Council of Higher Education are to encourage American youth of Czech parentage to acquire a higher education; to give advice and information to the Czech people concerning the advantages and benefits that the various institutions of learning offer the students; and to render financial assistance to those who deserve to receive it. Applicants for loans must be of Czech descent, have a knowledge of the Czech or Slovak language, and be of good moral character. A student who can meet these requirements may borrow from the Council and has a period of five years in which to pay back his loan without interest.[201]

In 1909 a report of the organization which was made in one of the council conventions stated that in seven years $2500 had been loaned to fourteen students. At that same convention it was decided to aid deserving students complete their high school courses. By the end of the year 1941 a total of $107,442 had been loaned to 276 students in thirty-two states.[202]

---

[199] *Přehled matice vyššího vzdělání*, p. 21. This booklet contains a report of the organization from 1902 to 1908.
[200] *The Cedar Rapids Gazette*, January 1, 1933.
[201] Constitution and By-laws of the Council of Higher Education.
[202] *The Cedar Rapids Republican*, July 27, 1909; annual report of the Council of Higher Education for the year 1941.

In 1904, in order to acquaint all Czech students with the culture of Bohemia, the Council of Higher Education established a movable library. This was made possible through a donation of fifty dollars from Mr. Severa and by contributions of books and money from other people interested in the project. All Czech students have been able to borrow from the Council, without cost except for transportation, volumes of Czech prose, poetry, and history.[203]

Americanization Classes

In addition to the Czech language schools, classes have also been organized in Cedar Rapids to teach citizenship and the English language to Czech immigrants. The first of these was started in 1904 when a group of young people asked Miss Sara Hrbek, a public school teacher, for instruction in the English language. Her first classes, which she taught without remuneration, were conducted in the Czech school building. In 1905, through the efforts of Joseph Mekota who was then a member of the Board of Education, these evening classes became a part of the public school system.[204]

The teacher who taught for the most years was John C. Stepan. He was born in Bohemia where he studied eight languages. After his arrival in the United States at the age of nineteen, he graduated from the Cook County Normal School and later studied in the University of North Dakota. In 1903 he came to Cedar Rapids where, for thirty-six years, he conducted classes in citizenship two or three evenings a week. From 1917 to 1922 he also had a two-hour class one night a week at the T.M. Sinclair Company plant. During that time his enrollment there increased from thirty-five to sixty-five

---

[203] *Přehled matice vyššího vzdělání*, p. 42.
[204] *The Cedar Rapids Gazette*, January 1, 1933.

adult students.   Of the 3000 immigrants who have been enrolled in Mr. Stepan's classes a large majority were Czechs.[205]
In September, 1938, a Miss Alma Wright was sent to Cedar Rapids by a federal agency to organize classes in citizenship and to prepare aliens for naturalization examinations. She was sponsored by the Board of Education, the ZCBJ, the YWCA, Coe College, and the administrative officials of the city. Two-hour classes in citizenship and the English language were organized. From that date until September, 1942, these classes were taught each afternoon and evening, except Friday, at the YWCA, the McKinley School, Coe College, the police station, and the ZCBJ Hall. At the latter place, Miss Wright's enrollees were Czech women who had been naturalized but who wished to perfect their speaking knowledge of the English language.   Classes were also continued through the summer at the Czech school and at the ZCBJ Hall, both of which places had been donated for the purpose.
The Board of Education cooperated by furnishing part of the supplies and by permitting the use of rooms in the McKinley School for some of the classes. Industrial plants such as Wilson and Company, Quaker Oats, and Penick and Ford showed interest in the project by urging their foreign-born employees to enroll in these classes. The enrollment for 1939 was the largest of all the years because, after the European war started, aliens in Cedar Rapids were anxious to become citizens. Fourteen nationalities were registered in the classes but over half of the total number of enrollees were Czech.[206]

---

[205] *The Cedar Rapids Gazette*, November 9, 1941. Information was also secured from John C. Stepan.
[206] This report was secured from Miss Alma Wright.   No citizenship classes have been held since September, 1942.

Libraries

The libraries of the Reading Society, the Cedar Rapids Public Library, and the libraries in the parochial schools have given the Czech people of the city access to books in their native tongue. The Reading Society, proposing to furnish the best possible books for its members and to promote a love for the language and literature of Bohemia, purchased its first volumes from Prague in December, 1868. During the ensuing years the Reading Society has maintained a library first in its own hall, then in the Sokol Hall, and since 1900 on the second floor of the Czech school building.[207]

Previous to 1938 the Reading Society purchased from two hundred to four hundred dollars' worth of books a year from Prague. Since that year a few volumes have been secured from Czech publishing companies in Racine and Omaha. Rather fragmentary records indicate that in 1911 the library owned 2500 books; in 1941 it had 5500 books, about twenty-five of which were in the English language. All the other volumes were in the Czech language but they included translations of Russian, French, English, Spanish, and German authors. A record of the circulation of books which has been kept since 1922 shows practically no decrease in the number of volumes issued each year. In 1922, 6273 books were circulated; in 1927, 6727; in 1932, 6073; in 1937, 6326; and in 1941, 6641. According to Joseph Holub, one of the librarians, these volumes were all issued to practically the same fifty or sixty people. All of the readers are adults.[208]

The Cedar Rapids Public Library also has a department of Czech literature which was established in November, 1907, with an appropriate ceremony. On that day three hundred Czech citizens came to the library to commemorate the Battle

---

[207] Brewer and Wick's *History of Linn County, Iowa*, Vol. I, p. 124. Material was also secured from Joseph Holub, one of the present librarians.
[208] Brewer and Wick's *History of Linn County, Iowa*, Vol. I, p. 252; information from Joseph Holub, librarian since 1920.

of White Mountain and to institute the Czech department of the library. One hundred and fourteen volumes which had been purchased in Prague were on display. Some were beautifully bound in bright red Morocco leather and the children's books were attractively illustrated. From time to time new volumes were purchased and added to the original collection. By April, 1942, the library had 1507 books in the Czech language.[209]

In 1915, two substations were opened in the southeast and southwest sections of the city where a large percentage of the Czech people lived and a Miss Kosek, who spoke the Czech language, served as station librarian. The southwest station reported that 69 per cent of all books issued to adults in 1916 were Czech books. During the years from 1911 to 1932 there was a marked annual increase in the circulation of Czech books. Since 1932 there has been a decrease in the circulation of Czech books and the report for 1941-1942 showed the smallest circulation of Czech books since 1910, only 616 volumes. It thus appears that the Czech library patrons have either read all of the books in that language in the library or that the present generation no longer manifests an interest in Czech literature.[210]

Two other libraries, the parochial libraries of Saint Wenceslaus and Saint Ludmila parishes, also have Czech books. The Saint Wenceslaus high school has some 500 Czech volumes, few of which are now read. The library for the Saint Ludmila parish on the second floor of the school building had, in May 1942, only twenty Czech books, but the

---

[209] *Annual Report of the Cedar Rapids Free Public Library*, 1907; *The Cedar Rapids Republican*, November 7, 1907; information secured from the annual reports of the library and from material furnished by Miss Edna Erickson, a librarian of the Cedar Rapids Public Library.

[210] This material was secured from the annual reports of the library and from Miss Ruby Taylor, one of the librarians of the Cedar Rapids Public Library.

library subscribes to three magazines and two newspapers printed in the Czech language.[211]

The Press

The first Czech newspaper published in Cedar Rapids was *Pokrok*. Founded in Racine, Wisconsin, by Joseph Pastor, it was brought to Cedar Rapids and published there by Frank B. Zdrubek, a militant atheist, from 1869 to 1871. It was issued every Saturday, had about 1600 subscribers, and at that time was next to the largest Czech newspaper in the United States. *Slovan Americký*, founded in Iowa City in 1869 by Jan Barta Letovsky, was moved to Cedar Rapids after 1872 and issued every Tuesday and Friday. *The Day*, which first appeared in Cedar Rapids in November, 1886, was edited by John B. Suster. Its contents consisted of Czech nationalistic material and advertisements. The next newspaper, *Svit* (The Dawn), published in Cedar Rapids in 1896 by F.K. Ringsmuth and Jan Borecky, had a large circulation among the intelligent and religious Czechs. A year later Mr. Ringsmuth also edited a newspaper known as *Listy* (News).[212]

During the early 1900s several newspapers appeared. *Pravda* (Truth) was published in Cedar Rapids from October 1900 to April 1902. It was a Catholic journal dedicated to the interests of the Czechs and Slovaks in America. *Česká Lípa* (Czech Linden) was published by Frank J. Tisera to take the place of *Pravda*. Three years later, from October 1905 to March 1906, a weekly paper, *Lidové Listy* (Paper of the People), was edited by Karel J. Sladek. In April 1905, J.J. Hajek edited a Cedar Rapids supplement of the paper *Svornost* known as *Věstník Iowský* (Iowa Publication). Since Mr.

---

[211] Material furnished by Monsignor Vojacek and the Sisters of the Saint Ludmila School.
[212] Thomas Capek's *Fifty Years of Cech Letters in America*, pp. 107, 135, 157, 191, 243.

98

Hajek's death, T.B. Hlubucek has edited two or three columns of local news in the *Svornost*.[213]

Frank Hradecky published the weekly paper *Humoroistické Listy* (Humor Paper) from April 12, 1906, to November 7, 1908. The next month the name of this paper was changed to *Cedar Rapidské Listy*. It is still published in the city. From 1908 to 1912 it was edited by Mr. Hradecky. From 1912 to 1918 and from 1931 to the present time (1944) John Stepan has been the editor. Politically the paper is independent. In 1928 it had nearly 3500 subscribers, about 20 per cent of whom lived outside of Cedar Rapids. Copies at that time were mailed to Canada and Czechoslovakia. Mr. Stepan is of the opinion that few young people of Czech descent now read the paper.[214]

Cedar Rapids Czechs and the First World War

The participation of the Cedar Rapids Czechs in the First World War was, perhaps, their most outstanding activity during the period from 1880 to 1918. In October 1914, a Bohemian Relief Society was organized in the city to raise money for the destitute widows and orphans of Bohemia. Even before a formal campaign was instituted, six hundred dollars was raised for the fund. Within the next few months, money poured in from the contributions of individuals and lodges and from the proceeds of plays and concerts.

On February 26, 1915, this local war relief organization affiliated with a new national organization, the Bohemian National Alliance, which through its local and state units worked for the liberation of Bohemia. The local officers were: F.M. Barta, president; Jan Pichner, vice president; Charles V.

---

[213] Capek's *Fifty Years of Cech Letters in America*, pp. 164, 167, 172, 173.
[214] Capek's *Fifty Years of Cech Letters in America*, p. 175; material from John C. Stepan.

Svoboda, secretary; and Jan J. Hrbek, treasurer. Cedar Rapids was headquarters for Iowa and four of the five state trustees were Cedar Rapids men. As a result of continued solicitations, $2700 was raised locally by this organization during the first year of its existence. That the people of Cedar Rapids were in sympathy with the movement is indicated by the fact that local merchants, in that same year, contributed an additional $10,000 to the fund.[215]

In April 1915, as a result of a plea by Dr. J. Rudis Jicinsky[216] for clothing needed by prisoners in Serbia, the Czech women of Cedar Rapids formed an organization for work known as the Včelky (Bees). Each Wednesday afternoon they sewed for the American Red Cross and each Friday afternoon they worked in the Czech School for war orphans in Bohemia and for prisoners in Serbia. Funds were solicited with which to buy materials and pleas were printed in Czech newspapers for worn clothing and shoes. Garments were knit for soldiers and civilians, 248 suits of underwear for Czech soldiers were made out of muslin, and twelve huge bundles of materials for war orphans were sent to Bohemia. These contained handkerchiefs, towels, bandages, new material for clothes, thread, underwear, stockings, soap, and new leather for shoes. The Včelky also contributed $150 to the Czech Red Cross, and $50 for the care of war orphans. Between December 16, 1917, and December 31, 1919, this organization sent twenty-six large chests of clothing and supplies, in addition to the bundles, to the Czech Red Cross in Prague.[217]

At the same time that the Včelky was at work, the Bohemian National Alliance was active in securing contributions for the Czech war fund. The chief source of

[215] *The Cedar Rapids Republican*, October 16, 1914, April 11, 1915; *Památník činnosti cechu Iowských v boji za svobodu store vlasti*, p. 16.
[216] Dr. J. Rudis Jicinsky, a former resident of Cedar Rapids, headed an American Red Cross unit sent to Serbia.
[217] *Památník činnosti cechu Iowských v boji za svobodu store vlasti*, p. 12.

revenue was the bazaars which were held in Cedar Rapids, as in other cities with a Czech population, during the fall of 1915, 1916, 1917, and 1918. All of the Czech organizations of the city, both Catholic and Protestant, participated in these bazaars which were held in the CSPS Hall. In 1915 the profits were $2,392.50, in 1916 they were $1,257.55, and in 1917, $10,800. The amount of money raised at the 1917 bazaar was exceeded only by the amounts raised at the Czech bazaars in Chicago and New York.[218]

Each Sunday during the months of September and October 1918, from twenty to forty cars of workers, known as the Flying Squadron, solicited goods and money in Cedar Rapids and the surrounding area. Contributions included such things as a wagonload of corn, live pigs, geese, chickens, cows, rabbits, vegetables, a bicycle, a colt, two forty-acre tracts of land, and a piece of real estate in Cedar Rapids. Perishables were sold at once and other products were stored until the week of the bazaar. It was planned for the last of October but, due to the influenza epidemic, it was postponed until Thanksgiving week.

In the meantime, the liberation of Czechoslovakia and the signing of the armistice added new zest to the occasion which lasted seven days. Czech bands and orchestras played every day. Everything imaginable was sold at booths and at one end of the hall were two paddle wheels where potatoes, livestock, live fowl, and rabbits were raffled off. Chances on the real estate were sold at one dollar a chance. On the evening preceding Thanksgiving Day, a dinner was served with jitrnice[219] as a special treat. Goods not sold at the bazaar

---

[218] *Památník činnosti cechu Iowských v boji za svobodu store vlasti*, p. 12; *The Cedar Rapids Republican*, July 2, 1918.
[219] Jitrnice is very highly seasoned liver sausage.

were afterwards disposed of from a store on Sixteenth Avenue. The bazaar of 1918 netted $30,200.[220]

Another important event during the war was the observance of the Fourth of July, 1918. In the morning there was the usual parade which was more than a mile long and which included five hundred Czech school children, some in native costumes, and other Czech groups which were always ready to march in procession. In the afternoon the Czech people assembled in Riverside Park to listen to a pledge of loyalty to the United States which had been formulated by the Bohemian National Alliance. Fourteen Cedar Rapids Czechs, who were unable to enlist in the American forces, volunteered to serve with the Czech Legionnaires. They were recruited by four Czech officers who had arrived in the city on July 2nd for the purpose of securing volunteers for their army. A total of twenty-eight recruits from Cedar Rapids were sent to a camp in New Jersey to be trained before they were transported to Europe to fight in the Czech army.[221]

Throughout the war the Czech people of Cedar Rapids not only worked for Czechoslovakia, but they also acknowledged their loyalty to the United States by their participation in the Liberty Loan drives and the work of the American Red Cross. Frank Filip, who was especially active in both local and state units of the Bohemian National Alliance, was also Linn County chairman of the Liberty Loan campaigns.[222] The Czech-Americans of Cedar Rapids also served their country in the war by serving in various branches of the American armed forces. The Honor Roll of Linn County lists 2541 men from Cedar Rapids who fought in the

---

[220] *The Cedar Rapids Republican*, July 5, September 29, October 6, 13, November 17, 24, 25, 27, 30, December 15, 1918; *Památník činnosti cechu Iowských v boji za svobodu store vlasti*, p. 12.
[221] *The Cedar Rapids Republican*, July 5, 7, 1918; *Památník činnosti cechu Iowských v boji za svobodu store vlasti*, p. 12.
[222] E.F. Prantner's *These Help Build America*, p. 30.

First World War. Of these, 474 or 18.6 percent were Czechs or men of Czech descent.[223]

Immediately following the First World War, some of the Czech organizations displayed their interest in the new Czechoslovak Republic. One of these was a project promoted by the Komensky Society of Coe College. This organization was composed of the students enrolled in Dr. Anna Heyberger's Czech classes. In the spring of 1919 several recitals and a "tag day" were directed by that society, resulting in a collection of $1800, to which certain Czech donors added $1000. The society decided to found a camp in Czechoslovakia for children threatened with tuberculosis. Dr. Heyberger was in Europe that summer and while there she formulated plans with the Czechoslovak Red Cross for the location and maintenance of a camp to be known as Coe Camp.

In the meantime, between June 10, 1919, and the last week of August, the members of the Komensky Society collected $3000 from individuals and organizations interested in the project. At the same time, Dr. Heyberger completed arrangements for Coe Camp, located near Tábor, Czechoslovakia. Four weeks after the project was started the first children were received at the camp for care. A corporation formed under the sponsorship of Dr. Alice Masaryk directed the sanitarium until 1931 when the management of it was assumed by the Czechoslovak National Department of Public Health.[224]

---

[223] A.F. Dotson's *Honor Roll of Linn County, Iowa*, pp. 20 ff.
[224] This material was secured from Dr. Anna Heyberger.

Czechs in the Melting Pot

Early Czech residents in Cedar Rapids sought to preserve their national culture. They made efforts to have their native or their ancestral language taught in schools, classes, and organizations. The Reading Society successfully sponsored Czech language classes for twenty years. Then a group of women in their Dámská Matice Školská, who had worked for years to accumulate a sufficient sum of money, erected a school building where children of Czech descent might be taught to appreciate a culture which they loved. In the two parochial schools Sisters born in Bohemia gave instruction not only in the language but also in the arts, crafts, and music of the country of their nativity. Persistently clinging to that ideal of the preservation of the Czech language for its cultural value, a group of people succeeded, as late as 1934, in having that language introduced into the public school system of the city. In Coe College classes in that language were taught for ten years and in the public schools they were a part of the curriculum for three years.

This effort to preserve the Czech language among the young people of the city has not been successful and the use of the Czech language is rapidly disappearing from local institutions. In four of the five churches where that language was once the sole form of address for all of the Sunday morning services, the young people have requested and secured the use of the English language in at least half of the religious services. In the Czech Reformed Church, where all the Sunday morning forms of worship are still conducted in the Czech language, Sunday school classes are taught in English.

Two fraternal groups, the Jan Hus and Praha Rebekah lodges, adopted an English ritual in 1921 by requirement. The Sokols have increasingly used the English language in their lectures, gymnastic classes, and the Junior Falcon group. Only in the lodges where the active members are adults does

Czech continue as a spoken language. A lodge of young people, Cedar Rapids Number 262 ZCBJ, has been an English-speaking group since its organization in 1923.

An attempt on the part of some of the Czech people to preserve their literature has met the same fate. Although the annual circulation of books in the library of the Reading Society has not decreased in the past twenty years, those volumes are issued to only about sixty adults. A small library at the John Hus Methodist Church closed years ago; scarcely any Czech books at the parochial school libraries are now read; and the circulation of volumes in that language at the Cedar Rapids Public Library has decreased rapidly since 1932. The importance of the Czech newspaper is also diminishing. In the early 1900s several journals in that language were published in Cedar Rapids; now there is only one. That paper serves the interest of the older people, but it is not read by the younger generation.

Changes have also occurred in other phases of Czech culture. A natural fondness for the drama caused the formation of several dramatic organizations which have always been a part of the social life of the Czech people in Cedar Rapids. In recent years, however, fewer plays or operettas have been presented. Because music and the Czech people are inseparable, numerous expressions of their love for that art have been noted in their bands, orchestras, and choruses. Today none of these organizations exists. Instead, the Czech people find satisfaction in concerts presented by others, in their folksongs sung over the radio, and in the music of their country enjoyed in informal groups.

Through their fraternal, social, and religious organizations, the Czech people have preserved some of their traditions. Many of their lodges and societies bear the names of famous historical characters and distinguished citizens of Bohemia. Under the auspices of these organizations the birth and death anniversaries of Jan Hus, Jan Amos Komensky, and Thomas G. Masaryk have been observed with appropriate programs. Historical events of note like the Battle of White Mountain and the liberation of Czechoslovakia (October 28th) have also been celebrated. Cultural organizations such as the Česká Beseda Club, the Minerva Society, and the Czech Fine Arts Association have preserved the music, literature, dances, and dramas of the Czech people.

Certain customs and traditions brought by the Czech people from the "old country" are disappearing; others have become a part of the cultural pattern of the community. The *dračky* or feather-stripping party, the Šibřinky and beseda dances, and the ZCBJ *pout* are still a part of the social life of the Czech people. The *dračky* is now, however, enjoyed only by the older women; the Šibřinky fails to serve its original purpose because few of the dancers now wear masks; the beseda dance has been revived as a novelty; and the *pout* is now chiefly a children's party. The Karla Masaryk Chorus attracts attention by donning Czech costumes.

A phase of the national life of the Czech people, however, which has always been evident in Cedar Rapids, is their food. Kolaches and other Czech pastries are sold in all the bakeries and food shops of the city. People who attend their bazaars are either served jitrnice or the favorite meal of the Czech people which consists of roast goose, dumplings, sauerkraut, and kolaches.

In addition to their cultural contributions, many Czech organizations have served other important functions. Early societies were nationalistic groups formed largely for the preservation of Czech culture; later organizations were insurance groups. The two Sokol units and the lodges have engaged in a certain amount of rivalry, yet in an emergency, like the First World War and the present world war, these organizations have been able to unite in a common and two-fold purpose. They have worked for the benefit of Czechoslovakia and yet, as loyal citizens of the United States, their first allegiance has been to this country. The Czech organizations have always encouraged American citizenship.

106

The native progressiveness and intelligence of the Czech people have been demonstrated in the establishment of their local institutions. Societies worked in independent groups, formed corporations, and erected their own halls. Religious organizations, with little aid from others, built their own church edifices. Czech people taught citizenship to their own countrymen. Thus the process of Americanization was never forced upon these people, nor did Cedar Rapids ever ask them to relinquish the culture of their native land. Gradually and naturally the Czech people have been assimilated into the life of the community and have become Americans.

During their residence in Cedar Rapids this group of people has contributed to the civic development of the city. That they have served well in administrative positions is demonstrated by the number of years individuals have held public offices. Because of their extensive ownership of property and because of their insurance organizations, the Czech people have given stability to the community of which they have become a part.[225]

In the cultural field the Czech people have also made contributions. For years their bands were the only organizations of that type in the city and as such they played for all civic affairs. While their choruses have sung principally for their own groups, still their organizations have presented to all of the citizens of Cedar Rapids opportunities to hear Jan Kubelik, Bohumil Kryl, the Bakule Children's Chorus, and other attractions of a similar nature.

Perhaps their greatest gift to the city has been their skill and industry. Cedar Rapids can certainly attribute some of her prosperity to their capacity for labor. Brought up on the maxim, "Bez prace nejsou koláče"[226] (Without work there is no bread) [*Editor's note:* Literally, without work there are no kolaches], the Czech people have been industrious and active

[225] Brewer and Wick's *History of Linn County, Iowa*, Vol. I, p. 121.
[226] Karl Stefan's *American Czechoslovaks Appreciate Free America* (Washington, DC: United States Government Printing Office, 1938), p. 8.

in all walks of life. Through diligence and frugality, many have become prosperous. It would be difficult to select the most outstanding Czechs in the city. Three – Frank Filip, W.F. Severa, and Charles B. Svoboda – have received the Bílý Lev (The White Lion) insignia from Czechoslovakia, a rare honor conferred upon Czech-American citizens for distinguished civic service. In intelligence and educational advancement, in modern fraternalism, in social and cultural achievements, in the professions, in business, and in industrial enterprises, the Czech element in Cedar Rapids has made remarkable progress.[227]

Martha E. Griffith
Cedar Rapids, Iowa

---

[227] Brewer and Wick's *History of Linn County, Iowa*, Vol. I, p. 126.

The History
of Czechs
in Cedar Rapids

Volume II
1942 – 1982

Assembled and Edited by

The Czech Heritage Foundation
Cedar Rapids, Iowa

Volume II

Part I

Updating Volume I

Pre - 1942
1942 - 1982

Prologue

Volume I, written by Miss Martha Griffith, covers the years 1852-1942. The volume includes the history of the arrival of Czechs in the Linn County area, reports of more than 109 organizations, lodges, groups, and activities, the names of more than 175 individuals, and more than twenty-eight different events – to name just a few of the details in the book.

Volume II covers the years 1942-1982 and has two parts.

Part I follows the similar organization and sequence of information in Volume I. A few reports pre-date 1942 and have been included. These are followed by the period 1942-1982 as the main body of the text.

Part II covers events and happenings that took place after 1942 – many of which are new developments in the Czech community.

It is to be expected that some events and groups have been unintentionally omitted. This is regrettable but understandable. Errors of fact no doubt will be found in the text because of the lack of written records and because memories are often vague about events that happened many years ago.

Volume II has been a volunteer effort of the Czech Heritage Foundation. We are indebted to those who so willingly supplied information and cooperated to make this work a reality. Bits of information came from different individuals, and we trust the readers and those who helped to supply facts will understand that it was the work of the Committee to compile materials from many sources for one item.

The Committee

Charles E. Krejci
M. Melvina Svec
Charles H. Vyskocil

July 1982

Banking

1942 – 1982

Bohemian Savings and Loan Association was still located at street level in the Sokol Hall in 1942. By 1946 the Association had moved to the present site at 320 Third Street SE, one block closer to the city business district. Renovation and remodeling the building was completed by 1947. Later two more remodelings and renovations were completed by 1974, making the present floor space three times larger than it had been thirty-five years earlier.

In addition to the spacious Home Office, four branch offices have been opened, one in each of the three quadrants of the city – southwest, northeast, southeast – and in Marion, Iowa.

Some 75% of the business is in loans. The Association ranks tenth in the state of Iowa with assets in 1982 of $156,536,000, which is more than ninety times the assets of forty years ago. The original Board of Directors and the founders of the Association were Czechs or of Czech ancestry. The present Board of Directors of nine members, with but one exception, are of Czech ancestry.

Information from John Vosatka

* * * * * * * * * * *

Iowa State Savings Bank was started in January 1906 in the southeast quadrant of the city. The bank was on the northwest corner of Third Street and Twelfth Avenue. Across the street was the ZCBJ Hall, and one block to the north the CSPS Hall. The neighborhood was a complete shopping area boasting of three grocery stores, a butcher shop, a bakery, pharmacy, two shoe stores, a furniture store, print shop, two dry goods stores, milk depot, Czech Library, restaurants, two theaters, some "saloons", a jewelry store, and the Fire Engine and Hose Company with horses to pull the wagons.

The Directors of the bank were: Frank S. Mitvalsky, Joseph Simon, Ed Hach, V.O. Hasek, J.W. Lesinger, L.L. Blahnik, F.J. Dvorak, John C. Petrovitsky and J.W. Pichner.

In 1917 the Iowa State Savings Bank moved across 12th Avenue to locate on the southwest corner of the intersection into the new building with its tall pillars of Ionic design. In 1934, the bank was reorganized and named the *First Trust and Savings Bank* with the same Board of Directors who continued to serve.

1942 – 1982

The *First Trust and Savings Bank* has been in its present building since 1917. Two additions were made in the 1970s; the most recent offers Drive-In Banking services under a roofed area. Additional parking space was acquired so the grounds now cover about 50% of a city block. In 1982, the assets amounted to $54,000,000. A branch bank was opened at 1820 First Avenue NE in 1972, and a branch bank in Ely, Iowa.

Dennis Hrabak

The *Citizens Savings Bank* preceded the *United State Bank*. The Citizens started banking services in a wooden frame building which was on the site of the present Granny's Attic antique shop. Within a short time, the *United State Bank* was chartered, 1922, and occupied its first Home Office at the southeast corner of C Street and 16th Avenue SW. At the time the capital was $50,000, and the surplus $20,000. It was a part of the southwest side Czech neighborhood shopping area.

The Board of Directors and founders of the Citizens Bank and later the United State Bank were many of the merchants and business people in the 16th Avenue community, who were: J.L. Prochaska, Charles Turechek, William Vavra, Jos. V. Zastera, Jos. Pechacek, Roy Jackman, Joe Kadlec, Stan Novotny, John N. Kucera, L.J. Pochobradsky, Sr., and L.J. Pochobradsky, Jr.

1942 – 1982

In October 1957, the *United State Bank* moved to its present site, the corner of Hamilton Street and 16th Avenue SW. The floor space has been enlarged twice and facilities for Drive-in Banking and parking now occupy more than one city block.

In 1977 there was a major change in the ownership and Board of Directors of the bank. In 1981 the bank affiliated with the Hawkeye Bancorporation of Des Moines as a unit of that group.

Insurance

1942 – 1982

The *Bohemian Mutual Insurance Association* after 85 years of existence still provides fire, wind and homeowner's insurance coverage for its members. The office continued to be located in the southeast business district of the city. The company has policies in line with the state laws and not the restrictions on insurance at the time it was founded. Bohemian Mutual serves Cedar Rapids and Linn County and adjoining counties.

118

Musical Groups

Several bands and/or orchestras were popular in the community prior to 1942. The following are some of the groups well remembered and even fondly recalled by some of our "older" generation.

The *Sbor České Tamburasu Zesna*, 1920-1924, directed by Charles Vosatka had a membership of seventeen players, two of whom were women. One played the tambourine. The other instruments from Croatia were stringed instruments which rested on the lap of the players. The name for them was "bugarka". They ranged in size from that of a ukulele to an oversize huge ukulele. Although the group played Czech melodies they also played a variety of other music. They were a popular group at dances.

John Vosatka

The *Fisher Concertina Orchestra* was one of its kind in this area. Joe Fisher and his father Frank started to play at barn dances in the 1920s. By 1930 the orchestra was established with eight members. The special attraction in the group was Joe Fisher's concertina, first of its size, custom built and LARGE while the other instruments in the group were conventional size. A concertina is a box-like "button" accordion, hexagonal in shape.

The group had a bus to travel on their tours over Iowa and southern Minnesota. One year they were on the road 364 days and nights with only Christmas Eve free! The music ranged from polka to waltz to two-step and modern. In 1933 the Concertina Orchestra was invited to the "Century of Progress World's Fair", Chicago. Fisher Concertina Orchestra cut records for Victor, Decca and appeared on radio WSUI, WOI and WMT. The men usually wore uniforms and sometimes "outlandish get-up outfits". One person who recalls the group most vividly said, "They were GOOD!" World War II brought about the disbanding of the orchestra.

Howard Fisher
Olin, Iowa

Kubovec Orchestra and *Dance Band* were active until the late 1940s. Members numbered eight to ten. The orchestra played at the Divadla (Czech plays) at CSPS Hall and the dance band for events at the ZCBJ Hall. The group was a popular ensemble and much in demand.

Irene Kubovec Dytrt

The Royal Entertainers were members of the Sedlacek families. The dance band group started in 1927 and over the years were popular musicians at dances and entertainments. On radio they played once a week broadcasting the familiar and usual "Bohemian" music. At one time, Mr. Eddie Ulch of the Solon Bank was sponsor for the group. By the late 1940s the six members of the group disbanded.

Henry Vyskocil came to the United States with his family in 1912. He and his brother had a band group in the Province of Bohemia. Soon after his arrival in Cedar Rapids, Henry started the *Vyskocil Band* with eight players. He had an old three-key trombone and his brother a clarinet; another member had a bass fiddle. Often when the group practiced the neighbors would sit on the porches to listen to the music. The *Vyskocil Band* often played at Sokol events. The Henry

Vyskocil bandsman was the father of Charles H. Vyskocil, retired president of the Western Fraternal Life Association.

The _RKO Orchestra_ at the Iowa Theater at the time of its opening in 1928 was directed by George Cervenka. Then in 1936 Cervenka organized a ten piece orchestra that was in demand for playing at Danceland and elsewhere. On Sunday the _Cervenka Orchestra_ played request music on WMT radio. By 1948, the competition of radio and the Big Band era brought about the decline of local orchestra groups.

Leo Cole's Bohemian Band is recalled by some people although no additional information was obtained about the group. They were active in the 1930s along with similar groups.

1942 – 1982

WMT Bohemian Hour followed the first of a series of programs under the direction of Frank Chramosta. For eighteen years, until 1968, T.B. Hlubucek was master of ceremonies. At these Sunday noon hour programs folk and semi-classical recordings, largely from Prague, Czechoslovakia, offered more that the "Beer Barrel Polka" and the "Prune Song" which had often become too much associated as representative of Czech music. A local quartet added variety to the programs. Many people sent donations to the radio station to add to a fund used to purchase food and clothing for the needy in Czechoslovakia.

T.B. Hlubucek

Leo Greco's Band is well known to many because of the radio program "Variety Show" since 1948. He and his band cut two records featuring Czech music and request numbers.

There were seven members in the band, playing country, pop and mod music. The band played live on radio 1951-1969. Since then the program has been produced from recordings.

Leo Greco

The Jolly Bohemians under the direction of Eddie Ulch were organized in 1977. They play traditional Czech polkas, waltzes, schottisches and two-step. There are six musicians. Sometimes they wear costumes if requested. They appear at Polka Festivals in states other than Iowa; play at dances, festivals and wedding receptions. Three records are to their credit.

Eddie Ulch

Czech Music and *KCRG Radio*. Ownership and management of *KCRG Radio* knew that Czech music was a "must" in the program schedule of their new station when KCRG took to the air in 1947.

The program began as a modest half-hour "Czech Melodies". For the most part, the program used 78 rpm records from Czechoslovakia. The offerings on the programs ran the gamut from Czechoslovakian opera to local vocalists singing traditional folk tunes in live performances.

There were several program hosts over the years including Charles Pulkrab and Joseph Svoboda. In 1953, the late Jerry Drahovzal took over the task. Mr. Drahovzal's popularity with the KCRG listeners was evident from the start and soon the program grew to a length of 2-1/2 hours, as listeners called "Bravo" and "More, More". The music during this period was for the most part from Mr. Drahovzal's own collection and included a few American produced records but was mostly from aging 78 rpm records.

122

In 1960 Mr. Drahovzal was joined by a Cedar Rapids native, David Franklin Kralik, who uses the air name of Dave Franklin. Under Drahovzal-Franklin the Sunday morning Czech music took on further dimensions.

The name of the program was changed to "Sunday Morning Czech Party". American produced polka and waltz music was introduced. Listenership grew rapidly. The number of requests for pieces suitable for anniversaries, birthdays, get well wishes and the like also increased dramatically as did the number of sponsors. The camaraderie between Mr. Drahovzal and Dave Franklin was pleasing to the listeners and added variety to the program.

During the next seven years, Mr. Drahovzal and Franklin enjoyed getting together every Sunday morning. With the microphone off while the records were played, the two discussed the events of the week and they shared their cares, problems and successes. The two enjoyed themselves so thoroughly, it was almost as if the program was of secondary importance. It was their friendship that was somehow conveyed on the air resulting in even greater popularity of the program.

In 1967 Mr. Drahovzal was elected the national secretary of the Western Fraternal Life Association so his co-host, Dave Franklin, took over the control of the "Sunday Morning Czech Party". The program continued to grow until it now occupies the entire 7 to 11 time block on Sunday mornings. More new music in both American and European styles is being added almost weekly. An extensive selection of German, Slavic and Scandinavian music has been added to the program.

Considerable emphasis is placed on the Iowa style polka music by Iowa polka bands. In April 1982 David Franklin Kralik was accorded the high honor by the Polka Club of Iowa of being inducted into the Iowa Polka Music Hall of Fame in the music-promoter category.

Czech music on *KCRG Radio* is more than thirty-four years old – in many ways a youngster and still growing.

David Franklin Kralik

The *Karla Masaryk Chorus* was formed in May 1937 to enjoy singing Czech songs and share the chorus works with others. The name Karla, or Charlotte, was the name of the wife of the first president of Czechoslovakia, T.G. Masaryk.

Esther Hronik Klersey, an accomplished musician, was chosen the director. She was familiar with Czech folk, classical and religious music.

1942 – 1982

During World War II, the Chorus appeared on the stage of the Iowa Theater with Edward Arnold and Frances Dee to aid Bond Drives. For the Voice of America the group made recordings which were broadcast in Europe. Several members made recordings for the University of Iowa Voice Department.

The appearances of the Karla Masaryk Chorus went beyond the Cedar Rapids area. Their programs were heard in Chicago, St. Louis, Rock Island and throughout Iowa. They were present at numerous anniversary events, conventions and festivals. For thirty years they sang at the Memorial Day events at Czech National Cemetery.

For the twenty-five years of the group's existence, Mrs. Elsie Volak Drahovzal was the accompanist. She was highly praised for her contribution to the success and popularity of the Chorus.

The Chorus has always appeared in Czech costume, singing in Czech or English. The remarkable thing about the group was that many who were housewives were taught to read music and to correctly pronounce the Czech words. Their love of music and devotion to practice gained for them recognition they little dreamed would come. By the mid 1970s there were fewer members in the chorus and less able to continue the demanding rehearsals and practice sessions. The group disbanded in the late 1970s.

Esther and LeRoy Klersey

Kolach Festivals

The first _Kolach Festival_ in October 1924 was started by John N. Kucera, hardware and sheet metal merchant, and other businessmen on 16th Avenue SW. The women in the community made the kolaches and donated them to the event. The following year the women were paid 20 cents per dozen and later as much as 30 cents to 35 cents per dozen! The crowds started to arrive in mid-afternoon. In the evening there was dancing to band music. The first year the kolaches were free! Thereafter a small charge was made.

The Festival was an annual affair. Later the kolaches were made by the Kosek Bakery and the Pechacek Bakery, both on the Avenue. Through the efforts of Lawrence Anthony, a grocer, the "Biggest Show on Earth", none other than the combined Ringling Brothers and Barnum and Bailey Circus, routed the parade from downtown south along Third Street to the 14th-16th Avenue bridge so the wagons and animals moved through Czech Village on their way to the circus grounds at 9th Avenue and 6th Street SW.

The Great Depression struck the nation and brought an end to Kolach Days on the Avenue.

However, the St. Ludmila Parish revived the project in the summer of 1931 on the church school grounds and continued the event until 1944 when the ladies directed their efforts to serving typical Czech meals at Hawkeye Downs at the All Iowa Fair.

1942 – 1982

The project of a Kolach Festival is now carried on by various church groups at bazaars and holiday events. In 1974 St. Ludmila Parish resumed the event as a three-day "holiday". More details are related under Religion in the St. Ludmila Parish item.

When Czech Village Association was organized in 1975, the annual Czech Festival in September brought thousands of kolaches to the booths and markets on the Avenue to the delight of the people who attended during the three-day Festival. The Festival is held the weekend after Labor Day on Friday, Saturday and Sunday. The Czech Festival is more than a feast of kolaches but a truly ethnic event which is described in detail under the title of Czech Village Association.

Compiled from reports by Alma Kucera Stanek, Charles Kriz and others

Dramatic Societies

The *Dramatický Odbor Čtenářského Spolku* (The Dramatic Club of the Reading Society) produced plays and programs in 1916-1917 when there was a revival of interest in these activities. The group presented dramas, operettas until 1930.

Two years later the *Dramatický Kroužek* (Dramatic Circle) was a response to the increased interest among Czech people who came from surrounding towns and rural areas as well as the city. Audiences filled whichever hall was the site of the production. From the orchestra "pit" came the music under the direction of Jansa or Kubovec. The Cedar Rapids Symphony Orchestra played on several occasions. Four plays translated into Czech from the English were: The Rose of the Prairie, The Count of Monte Cristo, The Bride from Bridewell, and Madam X. All were very well received.

Rose B. Polehna

1942 – 1982

During the 1960s there was a slump in the interest and the drama group ceased to exist because of the shortage of talent and likely expansion of radio and TV programs. Since the 1970s to the present, interested groups go by charter bus to the Chicago area to attend stage plays put on by the local talent and also to enjoy dinner at a Czech restaurant or gather with a lodge group. The Federation of Czech Groups arranges and sponsors these trips.

T.B. Hlubucek

The *Wednesday Czech Group* of twenty young adults meets weekly at the homes of members, presenting plays, singing Czech songs, learning about the cities of Czechoslovakia, read about history, composers, authors and Czech culture. This group merged with the Czech Fine Arts in 1933 after three years of activities.

Mildred L. Drahovzal

Czech Fine Arts Society, 1933-1946, had a roll call of forty members interested in Czech culture and heritage. Meetings were held once a month at which attendance varied from eighteen to thirty members. The group had well planned programs which involved many participants. The range of interests included such presentations as excerpts from "The Marriage of Figaro", Ronald Moehlmann's conducting an orchestra in "The Carnival of Animals", a trio performing Dvorak's "Donkey Trio", biographical reports about famous Czechs, history of Čechy, literature, history and the Fine Arts. The group also learned the national folk dance, "The Beseda", and enjoyed taking part in a large mixed chorus directed by Helena Kacena Stark.

When the society disbanded in 1946 the funds in the treasurer's account were used to purchase a large original Čermák painting of three Czech youths in authentic costumes. The picture was presented to the City of Cedar Rapids and can be viewed at the Paramount Theater for the Performing Arts on the second floor foyer along with other paintings.

Information from Lenora Stark Topinka

Education

Since 1905 _Sbor Dámská Matice Školská_ (Women's Society for Promoting Czech Language and Education) has been doing what its name means – support and maintenance of the Czech School. It functions in the nature of a PTA. In those early years, Americanization classes were held for Czech newcomers to the community. The class which graduated in 1906 was taught by Miss Šárka Hrbek. Twenty-two young adults were ready to apply for citizenship. Many people in the present community had parents or relatives in that class.

The regular six weeks summer session for pupils from all over the city had an enrollment of 200 during those early years. There were three age-grade-level groups taught by experienced teachers of Czech ancestry.

1942 – 1982

Over the years, enrollment at the school dropped. In 1951 the building did not meet safety inspection and was sold. After a year, arrangements were made with the Cedar Rapids Board of Education to use Hayes School on the southwest side of the city in the Czech community area. Class enrollment was around 100 for a five weeks summer session. Then as the years moved along, enrollment wavered between fifty and sixty pupils for a four weeks session. The competition with Little League Baseball, July 4th events, travel and vacation holidays by the families resulted in a dropping enrollment. It is of interest that today some of the students are of non-Czech ancestry but attend because classmate-friends are attending school. The pupils come from all over the city and even nearby towns and rural areas.

In 1956 during the Cedar Rapids Centennial, the program events were at Kingston Stadium. The first scholarship awarded to a high school senior was announced and presented. Since then as many as six scholarships are awarded annually; the number and amount depend upon the return from the investment of monies from the sale of the former school building. The scholarship is renewable for a second year at college.

The support of the school with the three age-grade levels and three teachers is maintained by the Czech lodges, churches and other Czech groups in the community. Graduation exercises close the session early in July with a program in which all pupils participate. The event is conducted by the Czech School Board.

Mildred L. Drahovzal

Matice Vyššího Vzdělání (Council of Higher Education) had as its original purpose (1902) to provide interest-free loans to student graduates of local high schools to help them to gain higher education. While loans are still available, a scholarship program has expanded the offerings. Also in 1924 the office was moved from Chicago to the Berwyn area. The present address is 8738 Washington Avenue, PO Box 134, Brookfield, Illinois 60513. [*Editor's Note:* According to their website www.cheonline.org, the mailing address is now P.O. Box 794, Chicago, IL 60690. A street address or phone number is not provided.]

1942 – 1982

The "Last Will" of James and Helen Hovorka named the Council of Higher Education as the beneficiary. Scholarships since then have been available (1968).

The requirements are the same for loans as for scholarships: "a full-time student of Czechoslovak background, enrolled in an accredited college or university in the United States, demonstrates high scholastic achievement and has completed at least one year of college study and in financial need." If the student majors in Czech or Slovak languages, literature, history and other related fields identified with Czechoslovak background, additional consideration is given. The student is expected to attain a bachelor degree or complete graduate studies.

The year 1980 marked 78 years of activities of the Council. Nineteen young women and twenty-three young men received interest-free loans for the academic year 1979-1980. The amount totaled $26,000. The total number of students in this category since 1902 is 706.

The Hovorka Scholarship Fund in its twelfth year has granted funds of $21,685 to twenty-seven young women and twenty-one young men. Since its inception the Fund has helped 524 students to the total amount of $249,590. Application forms for the scholarship or loan should be

130

addressed to the Council. [*Editor's note:* see www.cheonline.org for current contact information.]

Additional donations to support these projects come from various Czecho-Slovak lodges, organizations, and individuals and former students who benefitted from the "helping hand". Life members in the individual class total more than 200 of which five are in Cedar Rapids. Life member groups, societies and lodges total more than twenty of which there are five in Cedar Rapids. The writer knows from experience about Matice Vyššího Vzdělání having had a loan more than fifty years ago. It is hoped that recipients will pay as soon as they begin earning and perhaps later become annual contributing members. Modest donation amounts are gratefully received.

Compiled from the 1980 Annual Report
of the Council of Higher Education

Komensky Club had its start in 1909 at Coe College when eight students organized a study group to pursue Czech literature and history. It was not until 1912 under the sponsorship of Dr. Anna Heyberger that *Komensky Club* was the official name of the group. The Club carried out the original objectives of the group and set up a Coe Camp project in Czechoslovakia. Until 1932 Komensky Club was an active student group on Coe Campus.

1942 – 1982

The *Komensky Alumni Society* met in February 1955 to devise plans to use the earnings of the monies which had been raised for the Coe Children's Camp in Czechoslovakia. No funds would be released until that country "again becomes an independent nation." The value of the monies held in escrow amounted to almost $14,000. It was the earnings from this fund which provided for the establishment of a scholarship grant available to graduates of high schools in Linn County to aid them in their first year at college. Donations and earnings have increased the fund to over $20,000 by 1982.

At the start of the grants, one was awarded annually for a few years. The first recipient to a student of Czech ancestry was made in 1955 to Frances M. Chaloupka (Mrs. Robert De Ford Brown) who enrolled at Coe College in 1955. The sum was $450.00. She is the secretary of Komensky Club.

From 1955 to 1981 a total of 69 scholarships have been awarded. At present the award is $250.00 with five grants made in 1981. Consideration is being given to fewer awards and larger sums. Of course such changes depend upon earnings of funds invested. The award is sent directly to the Bursar or Treasurer of the college at which the student enrolls to help defray the expenses of tuition and fees. Over the last 26 years, the students have entered fifteen different colleges or universities in the state of Iowa.

Sokols

Sokol Gymnastic Association from its beginning until 1968 had the secretary's monthly report of meetings written in the Czech language. The records reveal the constant effort to maintain, improve and expand the teaching of the Tyrš System of exercises so that at large gatherings – the *Slet* or Tournaments – the participants in districts and national meetings all over the nation could present in unison the exacting drills, exercises and calisthenics. It is an amazing and thrilling sight to behold THOUSANDS OF SOKOLS in their uniforms executing their drills in magnificent coordinated movements on an immense field. At one time instructors from the National Office traveled to the units to advise, assist and coordinate the preparations for the Slets.

The arrival of Frank Machovsky and family from
Czechoslovakia brought about new interest and participation
in the offerings in gymnastics and other activities. He
supported and took part in community projects which helped
to perpetuate the culture and heritage of the Czechs. He was
active in Sokol Camp. Following his death in 1943, a search
was made for a competent successor. In 1947 an instructor
arrived from Czechoslovakia but he remained only two years
and then moved to Cleveland. Since then the gym instruction
has been carried on by staff members.

1942 – 1982

Sokol Hall dedicated 73 years ago (1909) continues to be
a solid and substantial building of three stories and finished
lower level. In 1948 remodeling included showers, dressing
rooms and a Club Room. In the 1970s more renovation took
place – new draperies, curtains, painting, refinishing floors
throughout the building and improving many facilities.

Over the years the reliable source of revenue was the
bazaar held at the CSPS or ZCBJ or Sokol Halls. Raffles for
poultry and other items were popular. A variety of Czech
foods were prepared and served by the Women's Unit. The
last bazaar was held in 1949 at the CSPS Hall.

The Sokol Camp (1931) was a popular gathering place
for all ages. By 1965 the decision was made to sell the
property because of the decline in the use of the facilities. In
January 1970 the camp area was sold to the Wildlife Outdoor
Club.

On July 3-4, 1948, a major Sokol delegation from
Czechoslovakia was hosted by the Cedar Rapids Sokols. A
gymnastic exhibition in the Paramount Theater was cheered
by an enthusiastic full-house audience. That year, 1948, was
the last year of the Sokol organization in Czechoslovakia as
the communist government took over. Nowadays what had

been the Sokol Slet is called the Spartakiada – communist version of the Sokol organization.

Twice a year at the local Sokol Hall the traditional and popular Czech pork suppers are prepared and served by the Women's Unit, Sokolíce Renata Tyršová. The event continues to this day.

October 20, 1973 marked the 100th anniversary of the local Sokol Gymnastic Association. A celebration was held at the CSPS Hall – a banquet, program of gymnastic skills, speakers and presentation of 50 year membership pins by president Jos. Pazour to members. The evening was enjoyed in social dancing and visiting.

The Sokol Bulletin, a monthly publication of the local unit, has appeared since 1946. It provides a continuing record of current Sokol history.

After 1948 Sokol units were located in many nations. The units are members of *"Sokols Abroad"*. This organization is having its 5th Jubilee or Slet in Vienna, Austria, July 1982. In 1976, the "Sokols Abroad" met in Zurich, Switzerland.

Report compiled by editor from notes provided by Jos. Pazour, Sokol Historian.

Sokolíce Renata Tyršová

Sokolíce Renata Tyršová, the women's unit, is named in honor of the wife of one of the founders of the Sokol movement, Miroslav Tyrš.

The war years of the 1940s found sixteen brothers and one sister in our nation's Services. The Sokol women made a "Service Flag" with seventeen stars. In 1946 shipments of clothing and food were sent to Tyrš House in Prague to be distributed to the needy.

The Sokols have kept alive their Czech heritage by presenting programs of gymnastics, demonstrations of quilting, lace making, egg decorating and cooking. Wearing Czech costumes added color and beauty to the events to which they were invited.

At the Cedar Rapids Centennial celebration in 1956, the Sokol units participated in many events with credit to the Czech community. The following year a series of television programs featured Sokol activities under the direction of Marie Vitek.

Over the years the Sokol women took part in American Red Cross activities, making quilts, bandages and taking First Aid and Water Safety courses. Their community interest is evidenced by making monetary donations to civic, community and national organizations.

Two events in the 1960s were of special importance. In 1960, Barbara Nemecek Benda represented the Women's Unit in Washington, D.C. at the presentation of the T.G. Masaryk commemorative postage stamp. In 1965 a commemorative stamp was issued honoring the _Sokols_ in America. At that time it was said that the national sale was the greatest of any stamp in the history of the United States Postal Service.

Two national conventions of the American Sokol organization have convened in Cedar Rapids, one in 1960 and a second in 1980 which also was the 80th anniversary of the Women's Unit.

In 1971 the Sokols participated in a two-month Festival of Czech Arts at the Cedar Rapids Art Center. On one of the Sunday special programs, the Sokol Gym was filled to overflowing as the audience watched demonstrations of gymnastic skills at all age levels. At the Art Center, the Sewing Circle demonstrated quilting. On another Sunday, the Beseda Dance Group was in action to the delight of the onlookers. Egg coloring and lace making were also demonstrated.

The Women's Unit has been represented and participated in every District and National Slet (Tournament) and gymnastic competition. For many years Sokols in the Province of Bohemia and later in Czechoslovakia held periodic international Slets in Prague. You have read a few paragraphs earlier about the changes resulting from the communist takeover.

The Sokol women take part in the Czech Village events such as "Houby Days" and "Ethnic Fair", Czech Festival selling kolaches, handicrafts items and helping at the Czech Heritage Foundation booth and the Museum.

The Board of Instructors had a Sokol Cook Book published which has proven to be in popular demand. The sales provide income to support gymnastic programs. Another source of income is from the Sewing Circle. Their main project is quilting, with orders from all over the United States. Libbie Stastny reports that since 1968 the Sewing Circle has worked on 240 quilts! Eight to ten women meet weekly except for a few hot summer days. Originally the charge was based on the number of spools of thread used. Now the charge is based upon the design and amount of work required.

Prior to 1979 most of the teaching of classes was done by volunteers. Kveta Vondracek Smith taught classes from 1952-1972. She had made a career of physical education, inspired by the teaching of Frank Machovsky in the 1920-1930s. Not only gymnastics were taught but Kveta added folk dancing and the beseda, the national folk dance of the Czechs, to the junior and adult women's classes. This program showed a marked increase in enrollment and gym activities which continues to this day.

Compiled by Kveta Vondracek Smith, Marie Vitek, Ann Libor, and Mana Machovsky Zlatohlavek

Catholic Sokols

Katolický Sokol, No. 20 was organized at the St. Wenceslaus Parish in 1910. Records show that brothers Frank and John Hac, both accomplished Sokols (gymnasts), were the main forces in the organization. *Catholic Sokols* were established then to maintain the religious identity of the church. The local groups met each week and participated in District competition. In 1921, a Women's Class was organized. The National Catholic Sokol Slet in 1922 was hosted by the Cedar Rapids branch which had sixty-two members.

In 1930, the gymnastic classes were discontinued and the Sokols assumed as their project providing books for the Parish School. To raise funds they sponsored picnics, dinners, bingo and card parties. Since the close of the Parish School in 1968, the funds have been used for church programs and support of the Czech School. Twenty-two members are on the present roster but functions of the Catholic Sokol are limited.

Edward R. Kuba

Cemeteries

The *Bohemian National Cemetery* was established in 1895 with seven Czech organizations taking part in the planning and management. The Board of Directors was selected from the several organizations. The officers were elected from members of the Board. That procedure continues at present. The fee paid by the participating organizations and other funds are invested in securities. The annual meeting of the Board is in January. In recent years the secretary's minutes of the meetings are recorded in English.

1942 – 1982

The name *Czech National Cemetery* was adopted by the Board of Directors in the early 1940s. Since the word Bohemian is not a Czech word, the decision to change the name was appropriate.

The cemetery entrance is marked by two brick pillars. Just inside the gate to the right is the Soldier's Field. There are two sections to the present cemetery: the tree shaded older section of 24 acres and the more recent Park Section of 11 acres to the west, where 8000 individual lots are available. Markers are flush with the ground. Large monuments are seen in the original section. The Park is landscaped with ornamental shrubs, bushes and trees. Roads circle the addition. The Columbarium was erected in 1953 at the northeast corner of the original section. There is no requirement about the ancestry of those who purchase lots or spaces.

St. John's Cemetery consisted of some five acres in 1870 when it was organized. The cemetery is located from 17th Street to 22nd Street on the south side of 12th Avenue SE. Families cared for their own plots and almost competed with one another to see which graves would be the best decorated.

A large cross with the Crucified Christ and two Angels was erected on the highest point in the cemetery. It was a place for visits and meditation.

In 1910, St. Wenceslaus Trustees in their deliberations decided to enlarge the cemetery to meet future expansion needs. They considered 70 acres to the east, owned by the Hedges Company, of hills and valleys at a price per acre that was considered too costly. To the north were 3 acres, level but costly. To the west was a pasture in the Ira Davenport estate at a cost of $2,500 for 18 acres. This property was purchased. The plan was to use two-thirds of the area for cemetery lots and with the approval of the City Council to subdivide the remaining one-third to be sold as lots for dwellings. The sale was completed in March 1911. The City Council was petitioned to abandon the streets on the cemetery ground.

Parishioner Frank Stodola supervised the preparation of the boundary fence. This project cost $1,700 and was defrayed by the sale of lots. The firm of T.R. Warriner, Civil Engineers, surveyed the lots. There were four equal sections. At the point of the crossroads a diamond shape plot was reserved for a future chapel. One section was ready for immediate use. It would be 35 years before the next section was opened; another 15 years for the third section to be needed.

Taking part in the cemetery project were Joseph Koutnik, John Viktor, Joseph Sindelar, Frank Biskup, Fred Proutkovsky and Albert Dvorak. A special committee included Joseph Lesinger, Frank Hac, John Hynek and Frank Sedlak.

The remaining one-third of the land was surveyed and platted into 41 lots for home sites. The sale price ranged from $100 to $325. Sales were slow. The payment of the final installment was made by the Parish.

In 1912 several parishioners formed the Slavia Real Estate Company which purchased the 41 lots for $5,000 and immediately proceeded to build homes. In 1982, the Slavia Agency is still in business! The same year, 1912, the new cemetery section was surveyed with lot markers installed.

In 1922 representatives of the St. Ludmila Parish were incorporated into the Cemetery Committee. Two members, Frank Shor and J.W. Lesinger, were from St. Wenceslaus and two from St. Ludmila's, John Viktor and Joseph L. Prochaska.

In 1924 lots sold for $150 cash or $160 on payments. This plan included "Perpetual Care". The older part of the cemetery is tree shaded and rises to higher points at the east.

A small memorial chapel of buff sandstone is located to the far right of the entrance gate on the lower road which encircles the cemetery. The construction of the chapel was completed in May 1939.

At the gate entrance on 19th Avenue are two brick posts. The left marker reads *Hřbitov Sv. Jana*; the right marker reads *St. John's Cemetery*.

Edward R. Kuba

Religion

1942 – 1982

St. Wenceslaus Catholic Church is rich in the lore of Čechy and to many is considered the finest example of Gothic architecture in Cedar Rapids. On the walls of the church are preserved old Czech designs in the murals depicting legends and tales relating to the martyred King Wenceslaus for whom the church is named. Medallions of famous shrines in Europe are pictured on the side walls: Hradčany, the castle on the heights overlooking the Vltava River and Prague; Charles Bridge, famous for the statues; Svatá Hora, the Holy Mount and site of the Blessed Virgin; a scene from Velehrad where St. Cyril and St. Methodius brought Christianity to Moravia and Bohemia in 863 A.D. The two missionaries preached in the dialect of the regions.

The ceilings in the transepts are painted cobalt blue with orange background of the medallions picturing Matthew, Mark, Luke and John. Around the windows are designs of leaves and fruit of the linden tree.

Through the efforts of Msgr. Vojacek, a high school was opened in 1921. Five years later St. Wenceslaus High School became duly accredited. The school closed in 1958 when it joined other parishes in building Central Regis High School. In 1969, the Grade School closed.

In the late 1950s and early 1960s the racial and ethnic composition of the parish changed. For more than eighty years the members were largely of Slavic origins from the countries of Central Europe. Czech language is no longer used at the services. Under the leadership of Msgr. Chihak and then Rev. Frana and now Rev. Trzil, the church is more community oriented.

The facilities formerly occupied by the Grade School were used by the Linn County Day Care Center until 1982. The church furnished the facilities; the county, state and federal funds supported the staff. Father Frana aided in involving the parish in HACAP, St. Vincent DePaul and the Metropolitan Office of Catholic Education. The present pastor, Rev. Trzil, continues to involve the church in community programs. His ability to speak the Czech language is helpful and meaningful to the few remaining elderly parishioners of Czech descent.

Mrs. Lumir Kopecky

Rosary Society (Růženecký Spolek) of St. Wenceslaus Catholic Church was organized in 1881. Throughout the 100 years it has met on each first Sunday of the month with the recitation of the Rosary in the Czech language. In observing their centennial, the membership was seventy-nine. It is the oldest organization in the Parish.

Edward R. Kuba

* * * * * * * * * * *

St. Ludmila Parish continued to grow and improve its facilities during the past forty years. In 1953 ground breaking ceremonies were held for the new school. Progress was slow as much of the labor was volunteer. The school was utilized as classrooms were available. By 1958 the building was completed. Today eleven classrooms, a large central library and an all purpose room, cafeteria and two offices serve the needs of a K-8 academic program.

During this period two students received awards of note. In 1961 Kristine Barta (Jones) won the 1st prize in the National Safety Poster contest. In 1974 an art contest sponsored by "Parade Magazine" was won by Ruth Skvor in the UNICEF project to promote understanding of the world's people. Her entry competed with 1500 other posters.

The first permanent pastor was Msgr. Francis Hruby who served not only the parishioners but the entire southwest community from 1922 to 1960. He died in September 1960. Succeeding pastors were Rev. Albert Zachar, a native of the St. Wenceslaus Parish of Cedar Rapids, 1960 to 1973; Rev. Robert Cizek from 1973 to 1980; Rev. Clarence Frana is the present pastor. All pastors are of Czech ancestry.

In the early days of the parish, the services were conducted in the Czech language which today is no longer used. Still in use is the Schaefer Pipe Organ installed in 1929 which at that time was the first of its kind west of the Mississippi River! The stained glass windows bear the words "daroval" (donated) in memory of the early Czech pioneers who founded the parish and built the church.

A project begun in April 1961 was the construction of the convent for the Notre Dame Sisters of Omaha who staffed the parish school. On January 28, 1962 the Most Reverend George Biskup, a native of our St. Wenceslaus Parish and Auxiliary Bishop of the Archdiocese of Dubuque, blessed the convent.

To provide easy access to the church for the disabled and elderly, a side entrance to the church was built in May 1981. A lift was installed for parishioners in wheel chairs.

In 1947 the library was enlarged to facilitate the use of books by both school children and adults. The library now houses some 9000 volumes.

His Eminence Joseph Cardinal Beran from Prague, Czechoslovakia, spent April 20 through 22, 1960, at St. Ludmila's visiting the school and having lunch with the pupils. He celebrated a Mass in the Czech language at the Convent.

After 1944 the Kolach Festival was replaced by the ladies serving sauerkraut, dumplings, pork and kolaches at the All Iowa Fair at Hawkeye Downs. In 1974 the Kolach Festival was revived and held on the church grounds during the second weekend in June. People come from the entire city and adjoining counties. During the 1981 Festival the ladies baked 19,848 or 1,654 dozen kolaches! The price of admission to the grounds includes a kolach and soft drink. Kolaches are also sold at the food booth.

Today, St. Ludmila Church serves the Catholics in the southwest area of Cedar Rapids and includes the towns of Swisher, Ely and Shueyville. Approximately 560 families are members of the parish.

Sister Christine Elias

* * * * * * * * * * *

Husov Pamětní Presbyterní Chrám (Hus Memorial Presbyterian Church) has the name of the frieze of the church at 7th Street and 9th Avenue SE. The cornerstone date is 1915. The new church in southwest Cedar Rapids was dedicated in 1973, in May.

In April 1890 the church became a part of the English speaking Cedar Rapids Presbytery of the Presbyterian Church of USA. In 1910, the church became a part of the newly organized multi-state Czech speaking Central West Bohemian Presbytery. Rev. Hlavaty convened that event in September 1910. This organization encompassed Czech churches in Wisconsin, Minnesota, Iowa, Nebraska and South Dakota under the jurisdiction of the Synod of Iowa of the Presbyterian

Church of USA. Following Rev. Hlavaty and Dr. Joseph Bren was Rev. Paroulek, born in Kansas and educated at McCormick Theological Seminary in Chicago. He preached sermons in Czech but the children's sermons were in English.

1942 – 1982

Beginning in January 1942, Rev. Zdenek Pauk had been at the Hus Memorial Church since the previous October, 1941. He held double services every Sunday morning, in both languages. The church membership was 190 of whom about 90% were of Czech descent.

Rev. Pauk served as Chaplain of the Iowa State Guard at Camp Dodge, Iowa. In April 1944, the church granted a leave of absence to Dr. Pauk so that he might serve as Chaplain in the U.S. Army. Although disabled in the Pacific Theater, he resumed his duties at the church in November 1945. His pastorate continued until December 1954.

The last Czech-speaking pastor was Reverend Joseph Havlik. He was born in Czechoslovakia, graduated from the Dubuque Theological Seminary and was ordained in the Hus Memorial Presbyterian Church in 1917. He served the congregation from October 1955 until his death in October 1959. At first Dr. Havlik held double services each Sunday: an English service in the morning and a Czech service in the afternoon. The morning service became increasingly popular so the Czech service was scheduled once a month. In December 1958 the pastor and his family moved to the southwest part of the city where a majority of the Czech members were living.

William Harnish, a native of Cedar Rapids and a graduate of the Dubuque Theological Seminary, served as student pastor from September 1960 until he was ordained and installed in March 1963. There were no Czech services after the death of Dr. Havlik. During the pastorate of Mr. Harnish there was a growing interest in moving the church to the southwest side of the city but no official action was taken.

In April 1967, Mr. Harnish was followed by Rev. Lyle Graff, a native of Bancroft, Nebraska. He graduated from the Dubuque Theological Seminary and was pastor until October 1971. Soon after his arrival plans were made to locate the church on land purchased at Schaeffer Drive and 29th Avenue SW. The former church building was sold to the New Jerusalem Church of God in Christ.

Following Mr. Graff, the congregation called its present pastor, the Reverend George B. McDill, born in Columbus, Ohio, and a graduate of the San Francisco Theological Seminary in San Anselmo, California (1963) and the McCormick Theological Seminary in Chicago (1977). When Mr. McDill assumed his duties in March 1972, the church site was already paid in full. In May, ground was broken for the present church building which was constructed on a time-and-material basis at the cost of approximately $192,000 with a considerable amount of the work being done by members of the congregation. The pipe organ from the former church was installed in the new building. The first worship service was held in February 1973. The church was dedicated in May 1973. On February 6, 1982 the church was free from debt – a mere ten years after Dr. McDill's arrival. The present membership of the church is 350 of whom about 90% are of Czech descent.

The *Tabitha Society*, the Women's group, was organized by nine women in 1913. By 1915 there were twenty-two members and today there are eighty-four. Since 1915 the Annual Bazaar – Chicken Noodle Soup Supper – continues to be one of the main events they sponsor. The society is active in mission and community work. Through various projects – rummage sales, quilting, craft and bake sales – they made a large contribution in paying off the mortgage of the present building. Originally they pledged $1,500 and in about ten years have contributed over $33,000! Tabitha contributes to

Linn County Food Bank, helps entertain the residents of Meth-Wick Manor and supports the Czech Village Association by selling crafts and baked goods at Houby Days and the Czech Village Festival.

The *Mariners Anchor Club* under the guidance of Dr. Joseph Havlik, then minister of the church, was organized in 1958 with twelve charter couples. The club "Cargo" (projects) includes serving at wedding receptions in the church, holding Chili Suppers, Pancake Suppers and recently Chicken-Noodle Soup Suppers. The money raised contributes to the needs of the church helping with the debt retirement, buying furnishings, providing devotional materials and hymnals, helping the Church School and giving emergency assistance to church families in need.

Rev. George B. McDill

At the *Jan Hus Methodist Church* during the tenure of Rev. Chada, Sunday school classes were well attended and conducted in the English language. The adult groups met at the parsonage; the lessons were in the Czech language. Most of the teachers were from Coe College and St. Paul's Methodist Church. The Epworth League meetings were also conducted in English. Two "Ladies Aid" organizations held meetings, one in Czech and one in the English language. During World War I the women of the neighborhood and church met at the parsonage several times a week to remake used clothing for the Red Cross to be shipped to Belgium.

One of the outstanding money-making projects of the Sunday school was the production of "Living Pictures". Another major project was the evening Christmas Cantata presented at Hayes School.

Upon Rev. Chada's retirement, the church conference appointed Rev. J.S. Lilley, a native of England, to the Jan Hus Church. Following Rev. Lilley were C.W. Harrot, 1933-36;

V.C. Grant, 1936-40; Clarence Oelske, 1940-41; Floyd Hillman, 1941-47; and Ruth Husband, 1947-57. By now the younger generations were slowly drifting from their Czech heritage.

1942 – 1982

In 1956-57 a city-wide census revealed the need for a Methodist church in the southwest quadrant of Cedar Rapids. In June 1957, Rev. John K. Moore, formerly serving as associate minister at St. Paul's, was appointed to Jan Hus and charged with organizing a new church.

The Jan Hus congregation decided not to relocate and so *Asbury Methodist Church* was chartered with its first worship service September 1957 in the Wilson Junior High School cafeteria with twenty-nine charter members, four of whom were of Czech descent.

On July 1, 1958, the task of merging 267 members of Jan Hus congregation with the 71 members of Asbury was completed. The Hus property was ceded to the Asbury congregation and sold. The Asbury group continued to meet at Wilson for a short time and then at the parsonage at its present location until the church was built. The cornerstone was laid in September 1959.

Rev. Moore's pastorate started with the Asbury Church project and he remained until 1964. Following him were William Cotton, 1964-69; Milton Vogel who served as interim pastor in 1970 when Rev. Charles Mehaffey arrived as minister and has been at Asbury United Methodist Church since 1970 – a total of 12 years to date.

The Jan Hus bell now hangs in the Asbury bell tower and the silver Hus communion chalice that is regularly used are constant reminders of the deep Czech heritage. In 1981, the Asbury United Methodist Church membership was 380 persons, 20% of whom proudly claim their Czech ancestry.

Community activities at Asbury are numerous. The major city-wide project is the Pautz Fellowship started in 1966. One hundred members meet the last Wednesday of the month except January and February. The folks assemble at 10:00 a.m. Individuals choose to take part in activities that change from time to time: working on bibs and lap robes for nursing homes; "Ditty Bags" for the Red Cross; bandages for the Leprosy Mission; items of clothing, crib quilts and other needed items for Hillcrest Family Services; stuffed toys, some going to Vietnam; comfort kits for the V.A. Hospital; crib quilts and infant clothing for the Rosebud Indian Reservation; crib quilts and scrap books that go to HOPE project and even more.

A short devotional service precedes the noon dinner which is prepared and served by volunteer women of the church. A free will offering has paid for the "living memorial" – the landscaping of the church grounds.

In 1966 at the first meeting, sixteen guests were served at a total food cost of $14.00; December 1981, ninety were served at a total cost of $180.00. Following dinner, a program is presented for about 30 to 40 minutes. Then individuals return to playing cards or bingo for fun or return to handwork projects. The costs of food and materials for projects are subsidized by the fund established as a beneficiary in a will.

The "*Quilters*" meet Wednesdays. Funds earned by their sewing help church needs.

The "*Circuit Riders*", a church youth group, started in 1966 with nine weeks of meetings in the fall and spring. Starting after school on Wednesdays, the meetings last 2 to 3 hours with the age range of youths from grade 3 to high school. Activities include Bible study, crafts, karate, trips, choir and other projects. Supper is served to forty or more

148

"Riders", many of whom are church members and often friends or neighbors of the members.

Information from Helen Chada
and Charles Jungman

* * * * * * * * * * * *

The *Czech Evangelical and Reformed Church* was located at the southwest corner of 2nd Street and 15th Avenue SW, and dedicated in 1910. As of this writing the church building is occupied by the Redemption Missionary Baptist denomination.

1942 – 1982

By 1959 the Czech Evangelical and Reformed Church again turned to the First Reformed Church with which it had been associated in the early years. At a meeting to unite the two congregations, the name chosen was *Eden Church of Christ*.

In the meantime, some Czech members had transferred to other churches in the city. An effort had been made to alternate Sunday services having Czech and then English language. The plan was not too acceptable to many younger folks so the membership declined as did that of the older members who had lived out their years.

After the two churches united, the ministers at Eden were: E.K. Schneider (1956-65); Donald McPeek (1966-69); the present minister, Rev. Glenn D. Hunt assumed the ministerial duties on July 20, 1970.

The *Lydia Circle* members continued to meet monthly for Bible study conducting their meeting in Czech until the late 1960s. The group made some quilts and sent financial support to the Children's Church Home in Missouri. As there were fewer and fewer members, the group met less often and looked forward to the summer picnic.

By the start of the 1970s the group no longer had meetings. As of 1982, three of the original members remained; the youngest was 84 and the eldest 94 years of age. By 1969 the Filipis had moved to the Good Samaritan Home in Quincy, Illinois. She died in 1970 and he died four years later.

Compiled from information from Leona Janesovsky, Rev. Glenn D. Hunt and Rev. Robert Elkin

Fraternal and Social Groups

The *Česko-Slovanská Podporující Spolek* (CSPS), also known as Česko-Slovanská Bratrská Podporující Jednota, the Czech Slavonian Benevolent Association, dedicated the CSPS Hall the year following the laying of the cornerstone in 1890. At the ceremony the Benesh Mounted Band, said to have been the only such group in the area, were astride their hard working draft horses.

Until the 1920s the Annual New Year's Dance was THE social event of the year. The Jansa Band supplied the music. At the stroke of midnight the national dance, "Beseda", started with ten or more circles of four couples on the dance floor.

1942 – 1982

The *Czechoslovak Society of America* became the name of the CSPS Lodge in 1933. Lodge Prokop Velký meets once a month. At present there are 150 members. Until 1960 the meetings and minutes were in the Czech language. Since then, English is used at meetings and recording of the minutes.

The 1970s brought more changes. Lodge Progressive joined Prokop Velký bringing an increase in attendance at meetings and activities. The lodge continues its insurance plans for members, and contributes to various charities and Czech projects in the community.

For many years the street level floor of the hall had a print shop, drug store, mortuary and the library of the Reading Society. In 1976 the building was listed as a "National Historic Site" and later was sold. Prokop continues to hold monthly meetings on the 3rd floor. A spacious ballroom with a Club Room, cloak rooms and bar were on the 2nd floor. Now the ballroom is used for gymnastic classes and the Club Room is used for social gatherings and meetings.

Early in 1982 the facade of the hall was sandblasted, sprayed a dark red color and tuck-pointed so the front of the building has been restored to its original appearance. The major part of the street level floor is occupied by the Service Press and Litho Company, owners of the building.

Mrs. Milton Stefl
(Emma Stodola Stefl)

* * * * * * * * * * * *

1942 – 1982

The *Western Fraternal Life Association*, formerly the ZCBJ, received an appeal in 1940 from the United States Treasury Department asking all organizations to conduct a bond drive to raise funds for war equipment. Several million dollars were raised making two medium bombers available to the U.S. Armed Forces; one such bomber was named "Spirit of Iowa Czechs".

Later on, the Association created a special fund and asked all lodges and members to participate. With those funds, twelve field ambulances were purchased and presented to the United States Army. An additional $250.00 was donated to the Schick General Hospital in Clinton to furnish a sun room. The balance was donated to the American Red Cross. One of the ambulances was presented to a representative of the U.S. Army at a special ceremony at the ZCBJ Park in July 1943.

Many members of the five local lodges served in the Armed Forces during World War II. The lodges banded together and contributed funds which were used to purchase items to be mailed to members in the Services in time for Christmas. Each package contained playing cards, pocket knife, hard candy, razors, soap and so on. Members were urged to send letters especially to those serving overseas.

The Home Office has always been in Cedar Rapids, Iowa. In 1959 the Association moved into its third location, the handsome structure at 1900 First Avenue NE.

For many years the lodges sponsored a Christmas Party for the juvenile members, planning a special program of entertainment and giving sacks of "goodies". In 1976 a family picnic at the ZCBJ Park took the place of the party. A noon meal and refreshments for all, games and contests for the young people with many prizes are provided. To date the picnics have been successful and more children take part every year.

As of 1982, the local lodges are: Cedar Rapids No. 262 organized in 1920; Hawkeye No. 423 organized in 1958; Mladočech No. 15 merged with Cedar No. 7 in 1969; Five Hundred No. 500 in 1964; Žižkův Dub No. 91 merged with Karel IV No. 13 in 1971.

The ZCBJ Hall, the second Home Office building, was sold in 1973 and the proceeds invested. The interest is used to support various charitable organizations. Contributions have been made to ZCBJ Park, Czech Museum, Sokol Association, Czech School, Lupus Foundation and the Lifeguard Air Ambulance of St. Luke's Health Care Foundation. The

152

committee meets annually for the purpose of making contributions to such worthy organizations.

At present the monthly meetings of Lodges Karel IV No. 13 and Cedar Rapids No. 262 are held at the Community Room of the First Trust and Savings Bank at 1820 First Avenue NE, Lodges Hawkeye No. 423 and Five Hundred No. 500, Cedar No. 7 are held in the Lounge at the WFLA Building, 1900 First Avenue NE.

At the National Convention in Cleveland, Ohio, August 29 – September 2, 1971 the delegates voted to change the name from Western Bohemian Fraternal Association to *Western Fraternal Life Association*. However, (ZCBJ) the Czech name Západní Česko-Bratrská Jednota is still being retained.

Charles H. Vyskocil

* * * * * * * * * * * *

Catholic Workman (Katolický Dělník) was organized July 1898 with seven members of the St. Wenceslaus Church. The members were: Jan Matus, A.F. Kopecky, Jan Kluber, Frank Simek, F. Marousek, Jos. A. Nejdl, Jan F. Pisarik, F.J. Kocourek and Father Kopecky. In 1924 the lodge had 44 members and held meetings every third Thursday of the month.

In the late 1920s the Catholic Workman and Západní Česko Katolická Jednota (Western Czech Catholic Union) merged. The new organization retained the name *Catholic Workman*. The local branch is St. George No. 45.

The St. Joseph branch of the *Catholic Workman* was organized at St. Ludmila parish in 1923 with eight members: R. Hruby, W.J. Drahos, Joseph Hartl, Joseph Kuderna, Melvin Kulis, Anton Parizek, Emil Proskovec and Vaclav Sasek and Rev. Francis Hruby.

1942 – 1982

The Home Office is located in New Prague, Minnesota. As a Czech fraternal insurance organization, there are branches in fourteen states. St. George branch has a membership of 67 juveniles and 359 adults. The St. Joseph branch has a count of 137 juveniles and 414 adults. One of their charter members is still among this group, W.J. Drahos. Supreme Vice President Edward R. Kuba has served as secretary of the Iowa State Council since 1930. The National Convention has been hosted by the Cedar Rapids branches several times.

Edward R. Kuba

* * * * * * * * * * * *

Jan Hus Lodge, IOOF, records reveal some astonishing facts in the past years. Costs for refreshments in the 1880s totaled $1.85 at one meeting; rental for use of meeting room 50 cents each week. After 1908 meetings were held in the new Sokol Hall. By 1913 the membership was 132 which kept increasing in the following years. Regular meetings were held every week in those days. The ritual was in Czech until 1919 when it was voted at the National Convention to use the English language. Special events, annual celebrations and conferring of degrees were held at the larger CSPS Hall. The World War I years found many brothers serving not only in the U.S. Armed Forces but in the Czech Legion. The Drill Team often traveled distances in Iowa to confer degrees.

1942 – 1982

Jan Hus Lodge had 485 members at its zenith. Meetings were held twice a month. The lodge was active in the support of the Retirement Home in Mason City, contributed to the

Scholarship Fund for young adults of families who were members of the lodge, visited the ailing and sick and attended funerals as a group. The meetings were followed by a program and social hour. The meetings continued until 1970. A decline in membership and activities resulted in an inactive lodge.

Fred Anthony

* * * * * * * * * * * *

The *Federation of Czech Groups* worked together in 1906 to participate in the semi-centennial celebration of Cedar Rapids taking a very active part in events.

Early in 1936 the Federation was organized to perpetuate the social and cultural life of the Czech people in the community. Meetings were held monthly.

1942 – 1982

In the late 1940s the Federation raised funds to establish a Soldier's Field near the main entrance to the Czech National Cemetery. A gray granite shaft or column rests on a base on which are inscribed the names of fallen soldiers of Czech ancestry in World War II. A floral piece is placed at the shrine on Memorial Day.

For many years, Czech Memorial Day was the first Sunday in June. A parade, marching band and program at the Czech National Cemetery and songs by the Karla Masaryk Chorus, the women in Czech costumes, and a speaker attracted hundreds of people. As time passed, the memorial observance was attended by fewer and fewer people. At present there is a revival of interest in the observance.

The Federation helped to relocate families who fled Czechoslovakia during the German and Soviet invasions.

When the Centennial of Cedar Rapids was to be observed in 1956, the Federation took a lead in organizing the events. The ZCBJ, CSPS and Sokol Halls were open for dining. A parade with Sokol Units and other groups took part in the celebration. Along Third Street in near downtown were booths with bakery and other items for sale.

Two of the projects the Federation supports are the Czech Summer School and bus trips to Berwyn, Illinois for members to attend the Czech stage plays and enjoy a visit in the Czech shopping community. Monthly meetings are the third Thursday of the month at which time a program, discussion and socializing close the evening's session.

E.R. Kuba and T.B. Hlubucek

The Women's Organizations

Over the years membership and activities in the women's lodges and social groups dwindled. As in many fraternal groups the younger adults had other interests and the attendance of older members at meetings declined.

1942 – 1982

By the 1970s Anna Náprstek, Žofie Podlipská, and Pomněnka Vlasti merged with the national CSA. The Karla Masaryk affiliated with the local CSA Junior American Czechs. The national CSA officers are proposing that the name be changed and voted upon at the Annual Convention in August 1982. To retain the initials CSA but broaden its appeal to interested prospective members, the name to be proposed is Consolidated Societies of America.

Henrietta Seabrooke

* * * * * * * * * * * *

Praha Rebekah Lodge #5 continued to be active at local, state and national events throughout its earlier years. The Degree Staff was invited to initiate candidates at lodges in Iowa and out of the state. At the State Assembly Conventions, one or more of the members held an office. In 1938, the Golden anniversary was a glittering event held at the CSPS Hall. Eighty candidates were welcomed at the regular meeting that week.

1942 – 1982

Praha Rebekah received state and national recognition of the chapter's leadership and officers and for starting projects still followed at meetings. In 1950, Praha Drill Team went to Kansas City where they made a colorful appearance in their Czech peasant costumes. Later, the same group was at the Des Moines State Conclave.

In 1958, the 70th Anniversary events were held at the Roosevelt Hotel when most of the state officers and all branch officers were in attendance.

In 1961, Praha again had an officer in the State Rebekah Assembly – LeNora Schuknecht. The years of her leadership were highlighted by special projects. The state lodges increased in membership by some 500 members. The same year Praha had an active part in the International Association of Rebekah Assemblies at Louisville, Kentucky. The Degree Staff conducted the initiation services for the candidates at those meetings.

Although the membership in this last decade continues to be more than one hundred, attendance at the twice monthly meetings is rather limited. The good works of the Rebekahs deserve continued support. They help maintain the Retirement Home in Mason City, Iowa, support the Eye Bank and contribute to the Scholarship Fund available to students from families of IOOF members.

* * * * * * * * * * *

Sbor České Vlastenky was founded in 1900. At one time the group set aside $5.00 for flowers for deceased members but now they send $10.00 annually to Camp Good Health. Locally it is one of the lodges that continues to meet monthly with ten to twelve members in attendance. Coffee and refreshments are donated by members. In December gifts are exchanged.

On May 6th, the anniversary, a special event is planned. Much of the conversation and social time are spent visiting in the Czech language.

Marie Kolda

* * * * * * * * * * *

The *ZCBJ Drill Team* was organized in June 1933 by Lodge Cedar Rapids No. 262 at the suggestion of Josephine Letovsky Kuba. She was then elected Drill Captain of the group of young women who performed at lodge installations and functions in Cedar Rapids and other towns and cities where there were lodges. The seventeen members met at homes for business and social evenings. New members joined the group over the years. Today, 1982, there are five charter members who have remained active for over forty years.

In 1939 the team went by train to Chicago to participate in the Czech program during the Nazi occupation of Czechoslovakia. The group appeared in a tableau entitled "Zvítězíme" (We will win over).

1942 – 1982

For almost twenty-five years the Drill Team represented several lodges in what is now the Western Fraternal Life Association. The team traveled to lodges in Iowa, Nebraska, Missouri and Illinois.

During World War II years, the group worked actively with the Red Cross serving food to service men and women on trains coming through Cedar Rapids. The project was financed by bingo and card parties, rummage sales and generous donations from the National Office of the lodge and member lodges, friends and members. When meat rations were low, the group donated the family meat ration allotments for the food project. Donations were made to the Crusade for Freedom and to the Ambulance Fund set up by the Western Fraternal Life Association (ZCBJ). The team participated in all of the War Bond rallies and parades. One outstanding event was the visit to Cedar Rapids of Secretary of the Treasury, Henry Morganthau. He presented the city with the Treasury "T" flag for excellence in raising funds.

In 1956, the Cedar Rapids Centennial was another special event in which the Drill Team took part along with the Czech community.

The COOKBOOK was so well received in 1956 that other printings followed. In 1963 some 3000 copies were sold in six months! The group continued their interest in making contributions to United Cerebral Palsy Center and Linn County Association for Retarded Children. These helping hands over the years totaled thousands of dollars to worthwhile causes as well as serving the people and sharing joys and sorrows.

The details in this article come from the forty year history of the Drill Team written by Libbie Melsha (d. Dec. 1977) entitled "Forty Decades of Marching Feet and Helping Hands." Libbie was a faithful member, devoted and talented.

The Drill Team will celebrate its Golden Anniversary in 1983. Meetings continue each month, weather permitting. The group will continue to be active as long as there is work to be done.

Vlasta B. Fajmon

* * * * * * * * * * * *

The *Nursery Auxiliary for the Children's Home* was one of the early Czech women's organizations which was started in October 1908 and is still in existence.

At the time, the "Home of the Friendless" occupied a two-story brick building at the corner of E Avenue and 15th Street NE. The children ranged from babies to five years of age. Dr. Wencil Ruml, one of the attending physicians, noted that some of the children were of Czech parentage and suggested to Mrs. Frank Hromatka, his sister, that several Czech women should form an auxiliary to help the nursery since there were not adequate funds to take care of their needs.

Upon the invitation of Mrs. Michael Houser, the following women came to her home: Mrs. Joseph Doubrasky, Mrs. Frank Hromatka, Mrs. Lumir Palda, Mrs. Joseph Pospisil, Mrs. W.F. Severa, Mrs. F.W. Slapnicka, Mrs. Charles Swab, Mrs. Joseph Swab and Mrs. W. Zalesky. Thus the Auxiliary was formed.

Membership was open to all women of Czech descent, fifty-five years of age or younger, limiting the group to sixty members. Their early projects and services included: mending drapes, clothing, baby cribs, bedding, curtains, and supplying jellies, jams, pickles and other edibles to build up the food supply for the winter. An annual picnic was held each June for all of the children.

In 1959 the Iowa laws were changed, prohibiting pre-school children from being raised in public institutions and were to be taken care of by foster parents. To comply with this law, the name of the Nursery Auxiliary was changed to the Girls Auxiliary of the Children's Home of Cedar Rapids, Iowa. Just previous to this change, the original "Home of the Friendless" also became "The Children's Home of Cedar Rapids, Iowa, Heartwood Treatment Center" to take care of teen age disturbed boys and girls.

In December 1979, "Heartwood" moved to 2309 C Street SW. On this new site are three cottages and one large remodeled "barn" with offices, dining area, kitchen and Board Room. The renovated hayloft is the gymnasium.

With these changes, the kinds of services of the Girls Auxiliary also changed. The girls at Heartwood and Maplewood are given birthday and Christmas gifts, ice cream, popcorn and other items not normally supplied, such as sewing machines, corn poppers, hair driers and sofa pillows.

The Girls Auxiliary meets once a month on the first Thursday for luncheon at Bishop Buffet, Lindale Mall, during the fall and winter months except for January. During the summer months the meetings are held as picnics at public parks. Husbands and friends are invited to the pre-meeting gourmet festivities.

The Girls Auxiliary will observe its 75th Anniversary in October 1983.

Eva F. Kouba

Libraries

1942 – 1982

Čtenářský Spolek (Reading Society). The Library's last location was in the ZCBJ building at 12th Avenue and 3rd Street SE. Fewer and fewer members came to the reading room or took books to read at home. Many books of value were donated to the University of Chicago and some books were retained by members.

When the building was sold in 1973 more than 2,000 books were stored in the basement. When Czech Heritage Foundation investigated the situation, the condition of the books had deteriorated, book bindings oxidized, paper yellowed, crumbling and not worth purchasing. As donations come to the Museum and Library a few copies have the book plate of Čtenářský Spolek on the inside cover.

* * * * * * * * * * *

The *Cedar Rapids Public Library* found less and less use made of the Czech collection of volumes and sometime after 1942 gave the collection to the Čtenářský Spolek. The present collections of books about Czechoslovakia are in English and cover a wide variety of topics and aspects of economic conditions, politics, and social changes since 1940.

Thelma Gover

* * * * * * * * * * *

The *St. Ludmila Library* at the school started with the purchase of one book. By 1925 the library was established with 800 volumes. Proceeds from programs were often used to purchase new books. By 1982 the collection numbered over 9,000 volumes.

Sister Christine Elias

The *Western Fraternal Life Association Library* collection of more than 1,400 volumes in the Czech language was catalogued in the mid-1970s. The collection covered ever so many categories, a few of which are: sets of encyclopedias, folio size reference volumes, dictionaries, art, biography, literature, poetry, novel, history, travel, religion, folk art, fine arts, music, science, children's books, magazines and others.

In 1981 this fine collection was given to the Czech Museum and Library.

* * * * * * * * * * * *

The _Coe College Library_ collection of some 150 volumes in the Czech language was given to the Czech Museum and Library in 1977. They will be kept as a separate collection as will the gifts from the Western Fraternal Life Association Library.

The Press

1942 – 1982

Of the eleven newspapers that at one time or another were published or circulated in the Cedar Rapids area, none is published now.

One major Czech newspaper in the Midwest and published in Chicago is the _Hlasatel_ which took over the _Cedar Rapidské Listy_ in the late 1940s. Two pages of the _Hlasatel Weekly_ edition are devoted to news of Cedar Rapids and Iowa. Under consideration is a plan to publish half of the edition in Czech and half in English. The _Svornost_ also published in Chicago was taken over by the _Hlasatel_ in the late 1950s.

The _Hlasatel_ has a daily circulation of 65,000 and 25,000 for the weekly edition. The more than 550,000 Czechs in the Chicago area account for the large number of subscribers.

Some years ago the _Hospodář_, published in Omaha, was a favorite Czech newspaper in this area. The contents were the main topic of conversation – recipes among the women, farm and garden news among the men. Stories of early Czech settlers appealed to all readers as did chapter by chapter of a novel – yesterday's soap opera. The paper is now published in West, Texas.

Czech weekly newspapers are published in Cleveland, New York City and elsewhere. Lodges, societies and organizations publish a monthly house organ, journal or bulletin in English with perhaps an article or page or two in Czech. There are also publications which vary in political viewpoints and interest – these have a limited circulation.

James V. Cada

War Efforts

The *Bohemian National Alliance* and *Včelky* were less active following their successful efforts during World War I, having accomplished their goals in aiding Czechoslovakia, the Red Cross and other agencies.

1942 – 1982

The approach of World War II brought about the reactivation of the Bohemian National Alliance but its name was changed to the *Czech National Alliance*. The Včelky did not take part as a group but as individuals they did their part in whatever project needed workers.

A group called the *Zlatá Kniha* (Gold Book) was organized in 1940 and worked for the duration of the war at the close of which they donated their remaining funds of $1,500 for rehabilitation in Europe.

The *Czech National Alliance* set up a plan to increase the membership and to organize local and state groups to help Czechoslovakia. The goals were to create an active propaganda project to free Czechoslovakia and to come to the defense of international democracy. The headquarters were in

Cedar Rapids. Within a year, the membership reached over 1,000 in Iowa.

Funds were raised by having bazaars, concerts, and card parties at the CSPS or ZCBJ Halls as events took place. In 1942 the Alliance raised $165,000, which was $25,000 more than the previous year. The money was sent to London to aid the Czech government. In addition, $47,000 went to help Czechoslovak refugees and $11,000 to the Czechoslovak soldiers in England, and $2,000 to the Czech and English Red Cross.

Dr. Eduard Benes made two trips to Chicago during those years. In 1945, the Cedar Rapids Symphony Orchestra under the direction of Prof. Joseph Kitchin gave a concert to celebrate the war's end. By the fall of 1945 the work of the Alliance was completed.

Southside Clubs

The *Sixteenth Avenue Commercial Club, Inc.* was founded in 1906 by a group of Czech businessmen. For years it was the dominant factor in southwest side politics. It once boasted of a membership of over 200 but as it approaches its Diamond Anniversary there are 42 club members. Originally it was known as the "Industrial Club of 16th Avenue West, Cedar Rapids, Iowa."

The objectives of the Club were "to encourage industries and stimulate business of 16th Avenue West and vicinity, to assist in encouraging private and public improvements in the locality and city."

The Club was incorporated on July 27, 1939 as a "non-profit organization under the name of 'Sixteenth Avenue Commercial Club, Inc'. The purposes of the new corporation are to be of educational, civic, business and social character, that is, the promotion of education, civic, business and social welfare of the members and the advancement of the welfare of the community in which it is located." Over the years the club has originated and helped support local and community projects.

1942 – 1982

Of the present membership, more than 50% are of Czech ancestry. The entire membership is dedicated to the objectives and purposes of the founders of the Club and the preservation and perpetuation of their Czech heritage.

Charles Jungman

The _Southside Commercial Club_ occupied the brick building at 1213 Second Street SE, from the 1920s until the mid-1930s. From then until 1955 the Lesinger-Polansky Funeral Home occupied the premises.

The Club was an active unit in support of the Czech neighborhood shopping and business district which extended from 8th Avenue to the 14th- 16th Avenue bridge on both 3rd and 2nd Streets.

1942 – 1982

Over the years the Club was active in civic and community projects. By 1980, the Club disbanded. Since 1966 the building is the home of the Moose Lodge.

* * * * * * * * * * *

The _South Side Civic Club_ was another active organization. The members continue to meet once a month as a social group. For some years the main event of the year was the banquet held at the ZCBJ Hall. The program honored high school athletes, teams and coaches. The event became larger and larger as the number of high schools and individuals increased. The project was later abandoned.

* * * * * * * * * * *

The _Cedar Rapids Restoration Club_ was founded in 1928. The goal was conservation of wild game and fish. In the winter free grain to feed the birds was given by the merchants on 16th Avenue SW to those willing to drive into the country and scatter the grain on the shoulder of the roads and highways.

When fish were stranded in ponds during receding flood waters, the fish were seined – game fish returned to the river channel and "rough fish" (carp) would be given away. During the Depression of the 1930s people stood in line to get the fish and there were always people watching the seining, waiting for the free fish.

In 1934 the club was incorporated as the _Linn County Fish and Game Club_.

1942 – 1982

In the 1940s the Club members planted thousands of trees on farm plots and park areas. That project continues and in 1982, 300 trees were planted at Pleasant Lake grounds.

After World War II the membership grew to between 400 and 500 following a membership drive.

Other projects were the raising of pheasants, some 5,000 on the Novak farm near the Czech National Cemetery on what is now Mt. Trashmore. Also raised were black bass in a farm pond near Mt. Vernon. The game and fish would then be released in their proper environmental areas.

At present there are between forty and fifty active members who continue the conservation goals.

> Stanley Kuta, George Svec,
> Paul Kosek and others

* * * * * * * * * * *

The *Railsplitters* were a baseball team in southwest Cedar Rapids in 1917-1926. Although the number varied, there were eighteen members most of the time. In their early years, the lack of uniforms did not dampen their spirits. They were a semi-professional team with their home base the ball diamond at Riverside Park. They played teams in many neighboring towns as well as the team from the House of David in Illinois and a local team called the Colored Giants.

The Railsplitters played for enjoyment and for entertainment. In addition to the excitement of the game, the old wooden bleachers might sway and even collapse as the team's rooters became excited.

The pay for the team's efforts was limited to "passing the hat" and whatever was donated would be their pay for the game. All players were Czech or of Czech ancestry. After 1926 the group disbanded. Some moved, some just drifted away as other events developed over the years.

> Compiled from conversation with Jerry Jasa,
> the "J.J." of the team

* * * * * * * * * * *

Volume II

Part II

New Developments and Events

1942-1982

Festival of Czech Arts

Festival of Czech Arts was held October through December 1971 under the direction of Donn Young, Director of the Cedar Rapids Art Center. A group of interested Czechs from various organizations and some members of the early Czech Society of Fine Arts (1930s) were the committee that helped to plan and carry out the project.

On Sundays special programs were presented to the public: folk dancers, gymnastic events, demonstrations of handiwork and handicrafts, Czech Christmas songs, chamber music, lectures, and a band group. One Sunday the attendance was clocked at over one thousand visitors and on another Sunday more than eight hundred attended the events and viewed the exhibits.

Throughout the weeks visitors viewed the exhibits in the Main Gallery. On loan were exquisite cut glass, ceramic ware, etched glass vases, an old violin, other musical instruments, an original music score, antiques, works of art, embroideries, laces, books and other items.

It is estimated that from the opening day, October 28th, Czech Independence Day, more than 14,000 individuals came to the Art Center. The Festival closed the 31st of December.

Soon after, people were asking if this project would be an annual event. Thus was started some thinking among a group of Czechs to consider a permanent project for the preservation of Czech heritage and culture. In a way, this led to the formation of the Czech Heritage Foundation less than two years later.

172

Musical Groups

First, to clarify the dates of the Centennial Year for Cedar Rapids: in 1849 the city of Cedar Rapids was granted an incorporation charter from the state legislature. Some historians say that the Centennial Year should have been 1949. In 1856, the state legislature modified the law regarding municipalities and Cedar Rapids took advantage of that change. Some historians date the Centennial Year for Cedar Rapids as of 1956.

At Riverside Park on C Street SW near 13th Avenue is a stone marker on which are carved the dates 1856 and 1906 to mark the 50th anniversary of the City Charter. At the Centennial in 1956, a plaque was attached at the lower margin of the monument with a brief history of the event.

* * * * * * * * * * * *

The *Centennial Band* was organized in the early 1950s and played at the 1956 Centennial event held in Riverside Park. Eight musicians made up the band. Carl Landergott, Bob Hach and Leonard Karasek were responsible for the organization of the group. The old uniforms of the Ben Jansa Band were in storage at the CSPS Hall and the bandsmen donned them with a flare – giving them a special appearance as they paraded on 16th Avenue SW, marching across the bridge and north along 3rd Street SE into the city's business district.

The members played in different band groups, one of which was directed by Ronald Moehlmann and another by Stan Vesely, both well-known conductors. William Vesely had several of the musicians as students at one time. One member had played for years in Ringling Brothers Circus, and another member, George Sigmund, played with the band until he was 89 years of age. Some members had a father who had been with various Czech bands in the area 70 to 80 years ago.

The Centennial Band enjoyed playing at wedding parties, public event parades and donated their entertainment to various groups of all ages and to organizations.

The *Czech Heritage Band* was the name adopted by the Centennial Band in 1977 at the time of the dedication of the Bandstand on the Mall in Czech Village. This was the time of the revival of interest in Czech "roots" of the community. Today Czech Heritage Band has eight members as in the original group. While personnel have changed from time to time, all members are of Czech ancestry and play Czech folk music with lilt and enthusiasm. Some of the members play in the Cedar Rapids Municipal Band and have done so for many years. Some also play in other band groups in the community. The Municipal Band members belong to their union and during the summer play at the public concerts in various city parks, rotating east side to west side on Wednesday and Sunday evenings.

The roster today includes: Bob Hach, Charles Jirkovsky, Leonard Karasek, Larry Klima, Carl Landergott, Rollie Raim, Jack Sedlacek and Marvin Sedlacek.

Compiled from conversations with
Carl Landergott and others

* * * * * * * * * * *

Accordion music. From the age of 4 to 12 Arlene Reyman played the accordion, mostly to please her parents. At that age and through high school years she was the "attraction" with dance bands on weekends. Later, she realized how much music with her accordion really meant to her, and the importance and value of her devotion to the instrument.

1942 – 1982

In 1944, at high school in Shueyville, Iowa, Arlene formed her own polka band. War years took their toll of members called into the Services and the group was disbanded.

Four years later (Mrs.) Arlene Reyman Boddicker left the dance band circuit to give her time and energy to teaching students and directing the accordion bands at Boddicker School of Music. One group was the Polka Band.

In the late 1960s a junior group of dancers was added to the project, now known as the "Boddicker Czech Showcase" having 12 accordionists, one percussionist, and 12 dancers. They performed in New York City in May 1981 at the Carnegie Recital Hall in the Youth Concert Series sponsored by the American Accordionists Association. In addition, Mrs. Boddicker has a professional polka band group, the "Polka Dots". They have played for many polka fests in Iowa, the local community and performed at Hancher Auditorium in Iowa City in the fall of 1981.

In 1949, the accordion groups became a non-profit corporation. They have traveled extensively in the United States, Europe and Japan. The "Cedar Rapids Accordion Aces" had appeared at the World's Fair in New York City, Osaka (Japan) and Spokane EXPO. This year, 1982, the Aces will perform at the World's Fair at Knoxville, Tennessee, as will the "Boddicker Czech Showcase". This latter group has performed at many Czech festivals in Iowa, Nebraska, and Minnesota.

The "Czech Showcase" presents a variety program of ethnic dances, vocals and instrumental accordion numbers. This group and the "Accordion Aces" appear in the community at conventions, lodge meetings, civic groups, senior citizen events, Camp Fire, Girl and Boy Scout events, parades, garden tours, state and local fairs, centennials at the

Five Seasons Center in Cedar Rapids as well as on local and national TV.

The members of the Czech Showcase range from 5 to 22 years of age. They are not all of Czech heritage but the present group is about 50% Czech ancestry. They sing Czech songs, learning the words phonetically.

The groups have recorded two stereo albums and have been requested to cut a third. The "Accordion Aces" have won many local, state and national honors over past years. They won first place in the national "Show Band" category in the Accordion Teachers Guild Competition for the past consecutive six years. They will try for their 7th win this summer in Nashville, Tennessee.

Arlene Boddicker

* * * * * * * * * * * *

1942 – 1982

The *Czech Plus Band*. A group of twelve musicians, most of whom are of Czech extraction and a few of mixed ancestry, has made themselves heard on the Cedar Rapids scene. The music of *Czech Plus* is in the traditional Czech style and tempo with a repertoire which ranges from the old compositions of František Kmoch to American Czech School favorites such as "Písnička Česká" and "Aj, Lůčka, Lůčka".

Czech Plus first appeared at some centennial celebrations. Among other engagements they played for service clubs, church-related festivals, Czech Village celebrations, weddings and family reunions. The group, formed in 1979, shows a constant improvement in the quality of their programs.

Under the management and direction of Wesley and Olga Drahozal, this band plans to continue to perform and entertain in this area for a long time, thus preserving the heritage that has been passed down to them from their parents and grandparents, and playing their part in transmitting this heritage to those who will follow.

Olga Sindelar Drahozal

* * * * * * * * * * *

Czech Language

Czech Language. In the winter session of 1974, a class of twenty interested students enrolled in an adult evening class offered by Kirkwood Community College. The group met once a week for a two hour session. The individuals were interested in their culture, history, literature, music and art of the Czechs.

The main objective of the course is to refresh the ability to speak Czech correctly and to study the grammar of the language. Many of Czech ancestry are now the third and fourth generation in the United States and want to preserve the language of their heritage.

Slides from travels of some of the participants as well as commercial slides lead to exercises in conversation and written work. The slides and movies not only bring the landscape a reality but also better view and understanding of the arts, crafts, handiwork, industries, recreation, the rural scene and many other aspects of life in Czechoslovakia.

A trip to Omaha to attend Smetana's comic opera, The Bartered Bride, was rewarding as was a trip to suburban Chicago, an area of large Czech population where they could shop, browse and dine.

The classes continue to meet one day a week in the evening during the college term at one of the high schools.

From material supplied by Charles Opatrny

Czech Language Studies. Czech Ethnic Heritage Studies Project was a response to the renewed interest by Americans in their heritage. Special funding was provided by Congress to establish the Ethnic Heritage Studies Branch in the U.S. Office of Education. In April 1974, the Grants Office at Kirkwood Community College invited representatives from the Czech community in Cedar Rapids, College Community School and the staff at the college to two meetings to provide guidance to grant writers, Pat Berntsen and Florence Masters, head of the Dept. of Foreign Languages. On May 1, 1974, there was submitted to the Washington Office a proposal entitled "General Ethnic Heritage and Specific Czech Heritage Curriculum Model Development and Field Testing, Incorporating Individualized Sequential Interdisciplinary Instruction."

Of 1,500 proposals submitted to the Washington Office, forty-one were selected for funding. Kirkwood Community College received $25,000 to develop the Czech Ethnic Heritage Proposal. Florence Masters was director and Beverly Garnant was assistant director. Ten people of Czech ancestry accepted appointment to the Advisory Committee. Also a curriculum subcommittee of ten people was appointed.

The nucleus of the project was a short play written by Ted Hlubucek about a family at their Sunday dinner. Dialogue from the play formed the basis for the language units. Video tapes were developed. Seven characters were in the play: parents, three children, an aunt and a visitor.

So many individuals and organizations became interested in the project that a monthly newsletter was distributed to 84 people to provide information on the progress of the project. Within four years of the completion of the materials, over 100 curriculum packages had been sent to schools, colleges, curriculum centers and individuals.

The Advisory Committee named Ted Hlubucek to serve as consultant on the ethnic heritage of Cedar Rapids Czechs. Dr. Zdenek Salzmann of Amherst University (Massachusetts) provided invaluable assistance and support. Ana Faltus of the Czechoslovak American Education Council (D.C.) maintained close contact with the project.

Florence Masters gave presentations about the project to the American Council on the Teaching of Foreign Languages, the American Folklore Society, the Czechoslovak National Council, the Central States Foreign Language Conference, The American Association of Junior and Community Colleges and was interviewed for a Voice of America broadcast.

The completed project was an individualized inter-disciplinary learning system for general ethnic studies utilizing the Czech language and culture. The level for experimental instruction was in grades 7 – 12 and was found suitable for resource material for elementary grades.

The curriculum consisted of 100 hours of instruction in language and culture developed from objectives based on a system of values determined by the characteristics and contributions of the Czech group. The materials were intended to add international dimensions to the educational system by blending of different cultures and developing sensitivity in cross-cultural understandings. The general model was completed by January 1, 1975. Six months later the development of the specific curriculum was completed. Field testing was carried out during 1974-75 at Kirkwood Community College and Marion High School.

At Kirkwood the Fall Quarter of 1975, Czech Ethnic Heritage Studies was offered as a 4 quarter credit course. Students could choose either the language or culture unit. Mildred Drahovzal and Charles Opatrny served as "native consultants" at various times for two years. Florence Masters was instructor-facilitator. In three academic quarters of 1975-

76 there were 49 registrants for the course. In three academic quarters of 1975-79 the total enrollment was 74 course registrations. In 1981, Winter Quarter, the Czech language was made available as a 1 quarter-hour credit to be repeated in independent foreign language studies.

At Iowa Central College, Fort Dodge, Iowa, Mary Cula Linney used the CEHS language materials in an evening class in 1981. The students were members of the Czech organization in the city and ranged from 18 to 84 years of age. The class of twenty-five people judged the course a great success.

The CEHS materials are still available from Kirkwood Community College. Frequent requests for information and materials continue. However, the Ethnic Heritage Studies Branch of the U.S. Office of Education no longer exists and so grant funding has ceased for ethnic heritage groups.

Material supplied by Florence Masters,
Kirkwood Community College

Cast of Characters *

Father............................ Jerry Drahovzal
Mother.......................... Vilma Nejdl
Daughter...................... Beverly Garnant
Sons............................. Charles Nejdl
                               Philip Nejdl
Aunt............................. Victoria Polehna
Visitor.......................... Ted Hlubucek

* Persons who appear on the video tape in the play at a family dinner in a typical home setting. (p. 177)

Czech Village Association

The *Czech Village Association* has its origins in 1972 when a small group of merchants on the 16th Avenue SW neighborhood shopping area, "Czech Town", met and decided to revive the Czech spirit and heritage in that concentrated area as a monument to early Czech settlers who contributed so much to the development of Cedar Rapids and Linn County.

On October 15, 1975, the City Council of Cedar Rapids passed a resolution which formally recognized the concept of "Czech Village" as proposed by the Czech Village Association. Thus the Village Association was begun. With the help of the Czech Heritage and Fine Arts Foundations, the merchants set out to develop the Czech Village Project.

Much has been accomplished in the renovation of buildings and attention to cultural influences. The next ten years were marked by many improvements and developments in the Village.

Merchants and businessmen along the Avenue dug into their own pockets for some $859,000 to renovate the heart of Czech Village. At least $700,000 was spent in construction of new buildings and restoration and renovation of the old. More than $150,000 was agreed upon in the form of an assessment to construct a new sidewalk-scape that would heighten the beauty and walking safety of the area and tie together the two-block long business section.

In addition to these efforts, the Association worked with the city government and the local citizenry in the Riverfront Neighborhood Committee to receive approximately $900,000 of Community Development Funds – money from a federal government program which provided grants for neighborhood projects. These monies built two new parking lots for the area, two pedestrian plaza walkways, the Riverfront Park development, the Riverside Driveway and other needed improvements.

Now a clock tower stands on an island in the middle of the Village, a deterrent to fast traffic through the Village and an added attraction. Two anonymous gifts amounting to $15,000 were made to the Czech Fine Arts Foundation for this clock.

Buildings that had deteriorated beyond repair gave way to Czechoslovakian designs and motifs to decorate stores, shops and restaurants. Piped folk music greets visitors and shoppers. Where once there were 48 metered parking spaces, now some 204 unmetered spaces fill the landscaped areas.

These Village improvements provide a pleasant shopping area and a place to "discover" for the leisure traveler. Czech Village is a living museum – specialties of homemade meat products, baked goods from century old recipes, saddle and leather products by folks who have been in the business for decades, glassware, ceramic ware, antiques, imports from Czechoslovakia, and handicrafts. In addition, the Avenue offers a variety of personal, professional and business services not only to the community but to the metropolitan area of Cedar Rapids.

During the year, four festivals celebrate Czech customs and traditions. The weekend after Mother's Day in May is _Houby Days_, co-sponsored by the Czech Village Association and the Czech Fine Arts Foundation. Mushroom Days feature Czech arts, folk arts and customs, Czech music and dancing, mushroom hunt contests and more. The breakfast menu features mushrooms.

Czech Village Festival, the largest of the yearly events, is the weekend following Labor Day in September. Featured are carnival entertainment, music, dancing, contests, flea market, "Bake-Off", kolach eating contests, a beer garden, a parade, and other fun events for children and adults. The Village Association and Czech Heritage Foundation make this occasion their annual celebration.

Czechs think red every March 19th, on _St. Joseph's Day_, Czech version of St. Patrick's Day. There is little religious significance to the event but a time to celebrate the day by honoring those with the name of Joseph! In Czechoslovakia the day was a community event for fun and merrymaking. In Czech Village the taverns serve red beer, the bakery sells red bread, the Village is decorated with red banners and a late afternoon parade is the main attraction.

St. Nicholas Day (Svatý Mikuláš) is celebrated in the Village on the Saturday prior to December 6th, the Saint's Feast Day. The legend of St. Nicholas is re-enacted when the angel and devil accompany Svatý Mikuláš as the three walk through the Village asking the children whether or not they have been good and whether or not they have said their prayers. The angel keeps the record in a book. This is the start of the Christmas season in the Czech community.

A new event, the _Ethnic Fair_, now in its second year (1982) occurs on the first weekend in June. Eight organized ethnic groups in the city participated by having booths, food, and dancers and musicians in native costumes. The enthusiastic audience joined in the singing and dancing presented by the different ethnic groups. Ethnic groups were: Blacks, Czechs, Danes, Greeks, Irish, Mexicans, Norwegians and Vietnamese. At this writing, the event is held in the "Roundhouse" – the Farmer's Market – just north of the Museum.

Information supplied by Pat Martin,
Coordinator, Czech Village

* * * * * * * * * * * *

Czech Heritage Foundation

The *Czech Heritage Foundation, Inc.* was organized in May 1973. Merchants on 16th Avenue SW business district were invited to attend the meetings of "Pride, Plan, Repair, Develop and Educate" at the Cedar Rapids Educational Services Center. The discussion centered on the preservation of Czech heritage and culture. As interest in the project grew, it became obvious that other groups needed to be organized to realize some of the ambitious goals under consideration. The present membership includes Iowans and others from more than twenty-five states and abroad.

The Czech Heritage Foundation serves as the liaison between the Fine Arts Foundation and Czech Village Association.

Among the goals are publicity and the promotion of events of interest to the Czech community. Publications include a quarterly newsletter, Naše České Dědictví (Our Czech Heritage); My Czech Word Book (ABCs); Meet the Czech Language; the History of Czechs in Cedar Rapids, 1852-1942 Vol. I., and Vol. II, 1942-1982; Album of Bohemian Songs; and Postcards of Olde Cedar Rapids. Also available is The Czech Book – Recipes and Traditions. A price list will be sent upon request.

The Annual Meeting of the two Foundations is the third Monday in January at 7:30 pm. The Annual Picnic is in August. The Board of Directors of the Heritage Foundation meets monthly. Members are welcome to attend any of these meetings.

A Speakers Bureau has a leaflet listing programs on a variety of topics: travel, customs, music, our heritage, the Museum and Library, art works and others. In addition, Units from the project *"Educational Kit"* are available on loan for display or for programs. From time to time additional events, meetings and programs are planned. For information about membership, programs, speakers, the kit or publications, write

Czech Heritage Foundation, P.O. Box 8476, Cedar Rapids, Iowa 52408. [*Editor's Note:* This mailing address is current as of 2012. See www.czechheritagefoundation.com.]

* * * * * * * * * * * *

Czech Fine Arts Foundation

The *Czech Fine Arts Foundation, Inc.* was organized in late 1974 to preserve and promote Czech cultural arts. The Foundation participates in festivals, ethnic fairs and other fine arts events. The Foundation has the care and management of the Museum and Library at 10 16th Avenue SW in Czech Village, Cedar Rapids, Iowa.

The Museum was established in 1978. The collection of authentic costumes (kroje) from different regions of Czechoslovakia is one of the largest in the United States. Displays include cut glass, ruby glass, porcelains, ceramic ware, works of art, pictures, handicrafts and tools. During the year the displays are changed; fall-winter displays give way to those of spring and summer.

The Library contains some 4,000 volumes, predominately in the Czech language. The collection includes books on fine arts, literature, poetry, history, music, folk arts, biography, travel, religion, children's books, encyclopedia sets, newspapers, magazines, almanacs and other titles. Arrangements can be made for research projects using the volumes. The books are not available for circulation. Later on, duplicate copies will be available on loan.

From 1978 through 1981 more than 10,000 visitors have toured the Museum. During special fairs and festivals the Museum has extended open hours. Tours may be arranged for groups and visitors. [*Editor's Note:* This facility is now the National Czech & Slovak Museum & Library. See the website www.ncsml.org for more information.]

The Board of Directors meets monthly at the Museum. Donations to the Museum and Library of cash or objects are income tax deductible. The Fine Arts Foundation has tax exempt status as does the Czech Heritage Foundation.

Appendix

Celebrations, Events, & Festivals
All Iowa Fair, Hawkeye Downs
Birthdays
Cedar Rapids Centennial
Cedar Rapids Semi-centennial
Czech Village Festival
Ethnic Fair
Festival of Czech Arts
Houby Days
Kolach Days
Kolach Festival
Patriotic Events
Political Events
Pout
St. Joseph's Day
St. Nicholas Day
  Svatý Mikuláš
Šibřinky
Social Events

Cemeteries
Bohemian National Cemetery
Czech National Cemetery
Columbarium
St. John's Cemetery

Churches & Religious Groups
Churches
  Asbury Methodist Church
  Bohemian Tabernacle
  Czech Evangelical Church
  Czech Evangelical and
    Reformed Church
  Czech Reformed Church
  Eden Church of Christ
  Epworth Mission
  First Congregational Church
  First Presbyterian Church
  First Reformed Church
  Fourth Presbyterian Church

Churches, cont'd.
  Hope Mission Chapel
  Hus Memorial Presbyterian
    Church
  Immaculate Conception
    Church
  Jan (John) Hus Methodist
    Church
  New Jerusalem Church of God
    In Christ
  Redemption Missionary
    Baptist Church
  St. Ludmila Catholic Church
  St. Mary's Catholic Church
  St. Paul's Methodist Church
  St. Paul's Methodist Episcopal
    Church
  St. Wenceslaus Catholic
    Church
  Second Evangelical Church
  Second Presbyterian Church
  Third Presbyterian Church
  Unitarian Church
Religious Groups
  Bohemian Brethren
  Calvinists
  Free-thinkers
  Lutherans
  Moravian Brethren

Cities & Towns
United States
  Berwyn, Illinois
  Brookfield, Illinois
  Caledonia, Wisconsin
  Camp Dodge, Iowa
  Cedar Rapids, Iowa
  Center Point, Iowa
  Chicago, Illinois
  Cleveland, Ohio

189

Education Boards & Institutions
Cedar Rapids Board of
Education
Central Regis High School
Coe College
College Community School
District
Council of Higher Education
Matice Vyššího Vzdělání
Czech School
Dámská Matice Školská
Matice Školská
Hayes School
Kirkwood Community College
Metropolitan Office of Catholic
Education
St. Ludmila School
St. Wenceslaus School

Fraternal Groups
Catholic Workman
Katolický Dělník
St. George Branch
St. Joseph Branch
České Vlastenky
Česko-Slovanská Podporující
Spolek/Spolku (CSPS)
Karel IV Lodge 77
Karla Masaryk Lodge 344
Mladočech Lodge 82
Progressive Lodge
Prokop Velký Lodge 46
Czechoslovak Society of
America (CSA)
Progressive Lodge
Prokop Velký Lodge
Jan Hus Odd Fellows (IOOF)
Lodge
Jan Hus Odd Fellows (IOOF)
Retirement Home
Jednota Českých Dam (JCD)
Anna Náprstek Lodge 24
Českých Vlastenek Lodge 1

Fraternal Groups, cont'd
Pomněnka Vlasti Lodge
Žofie Podlipská Lodge 25
Moose Lodge
Praha Rebekah Lodges
Praha Rebekah Degree Staff
Praha Rebekah Drill Team
Sesterská Podporující Jednota
(SPJ)
Hvězda Pokroku Lodge 4
Zdenka Havlicek Lodge 23
Western Czech Catholic
Union
Western Fraternal Life
Association (WFLA)
Cedar Lodge 7
Cedar Rapids Lodge 262
Five Hundred Lodge 500
Hawkeye Lodge 423
Karel IV Lodge 13
Mladočech Lodge 15
Žižkův Dub Lodge 91
Women's Organizations
České Vlastenky
Česko-Slovanská Podporující
Spolek/Spolku (CSPS)
Karla Masaryk Lodge 344
Jednota Českých Dam (JCD)
Anna Náprstek Lodge 24
Českých Vlastenek Lodge 1
Pomněnka Vlasti Lodge
Žofie Podlipská Lodge 25
Praha Rebekah Lodges
Praha Rebekah Degree Staff
Praha Rebekah Drill Team
Sesterská Podporující Jednota
(SPJ)
Hvězda Pokroku Lodge 4
Zdenka Havlicek Lodge 23
Včelky

Index

Czech Heritage
  Foundation, 135, 161,
  171, 181, 183–84, 185
  Educational Kit, 183
  Publications, 183
  Speakers Bureau, 183
Czech Home Guard, WW
  II, 58
Czech Language Classes,
  86–91, 103, 176, 177–79
Czech
  Legion/Legionnaires,
  101, 153
Czech Library. *See*
  Reading Society Library
Czech Museum and
  Library, 161, 162, 184–
  85
Czech National Alliance,
  47–49, 163–64, *See*
  Bohemian National
  Alliance
Czech National Cemetery,
  137, 154, *See* Bohemian
  National Cemetery
Czech National Lodge. *See*
  České Vlastenky
Czech Plus Band, 175–76
Czech Reformed Church,
  49, 67–69, 73–74, 103
Czech School, 30, 37, 88–
  89, 127–28, 136, 151,
  155, 175, *See* Dámská
  Matice Školská

Czech Society of Fine Arts.
  See Czech Fine Arts
  Society
Czech Village, 124, 135,
  173, 175, 180–82, 184
Czech Village Association,
  125, 145, 180–82, 183
Czech Village Festivals,
  125, 135, 145, 181–82
Czech Village Mall, 173
Czechoslovak Society of
  America (CSA), 79, 149
Czechoslovakia, 15, 48, 79,
  98, 100, 101, 102, 105,
  107, 120, 121, 123, 130,
  132, 135, 154, 157, 161,
  163, 176, 182, 184
Dámská Matice Školská,
  87–89, 103, 127–28, *See*
  Czech School
Danceland, 120
Davenport, Ira, 137
Day, The, 97
DeCastello, Rev. R.N., 72
Depression of 1930s, 166,
  See Great Depression
Dolezal, Vaclav, 33
Dostal, 17
Dračky, 25, 105
Drahos, W.J., 152
Drahovzal, Elsie Volak,
  123
Drahovzal, Jerry, 121–22,
  179
Drahovzal, Mildred L.,
  126, 128, 178

205

Nejdl, Jos. A., 152
Nejdl, Philip, 179
Nejdl, Vilma, 179
New Jerusalem Church of God in Christ, 144
New Prague, Minnesota, 153
New York City, 75, 163, 174
New York City World's Fair, 174
Notre Dame Sisters. *See* Sisters De Notre Dame
Novak, Rudolph, 58
Novotny, Stan, 117
Nursery Auxiliary for the Children's Home, 159, *See* Girls Auxiliary of the Children's Home
Occupations, 18–19, 21–23, 25–30, 31–32, *See* Professions
Odd Fellows (IOOF). *See* Jan Hus Odd Fellows (IOOF) Lodge
Oelske, Clarence, 146
Olin, Iowa, 119
Omaha, Nebraska, 58, 67, 83, 95, 141, 162, 176
Opatrny, Charles, 177, 178
Organ C.S.P.S., 78
Osaka World's Fair, 174
Paidar, Rose, 57
Paine, Thomas, 37, 61, 62
Palda, L.J., 31, 61–62
Palda, Mrs. Lumir, 159

Paramount Theater, 127, 132
Parizek, Anton, 152
Paroulek, Rev. Benjamin, 71, 143
Pastor, Joseph, 97
Patriotic Events, 24, 30–31, 40, 47–49, 57–59, 100–102
Pauk, Rev. Zdenek, 71, 143
Pautz Fellowship, 147
Pavlicek, 88
Pazour, Jos., 133
Pechacek Bakery, 124
Pechacek, Jos., 117
Petrovitsky, John, 23
Petrovitsky, John C., 116
Philipse, Frederick, 13
Pichner, J.W., 116
Pichner, Jan, 98
Pirkl Orchestra, 39
Pirkl, Frank, 39
Pisarik, Jan F., 152
Pochobradsky, L.J., Jr., 117
Pochobradsky, L.J., Sr., 117
Pochobradsky, Louis J., 29
Podlipská, Žofie, 81
Pokrok, 22, 60–61, 97
Polak, Jakub, 60
Polansky, Karel, 50, 52
Polehna, Rose B., 126
Polehna, Victoria, 179

212

37383922R00120

Made in the USA
Middletown, DE
02 December 2016